MAKE UP YOUR MIND

A Classroom Guide to 10 Age-Old Debates

Clark G. Porter, Ph.D.

With James M. Girsch, Ph.D.

Routledge
Taylor & Francis Group

NEW YORK AND LONDON

First published 2011 by Prufrock Press Inc.

Published 2021 by Routledge
605 Third Avenue, New York, NY 10017
2 Park Square, Milton Park, Abingdon, Oxon OX14 4RN

Routledge is an imprint of the Taylor & Francis Group, an informa business

Copyright © 2011 by Taylor & Francis.

Edited by Sarah Morrison

Cover Design by Raquel Trevino
Layout Design by Marjorie Parker

ISBN 13: 978-1-59363-714-9 (pbk)

To Sharon . . .
mi media naranja.

CONTENTS

CONTENTS

Acknowledgments

First, I would like to express my gratitude to my wife, Sharon, my parents, Audrey and P. J. Porter, and my sons, Ben and Jake. I could not have embarked on a project like this without their unwavering support.

A special paragraph must be devoted to my friend and colleague Jim Girsch, who has been blessed with a remarkable intellect and keen editorial skills. Without his help, this book would still be a disheveled manuscript in a plastic file crate.

I also wish to thank others who have shown a special interest in my efforts to complete this book, namely Carol and Earl Will, Scott Taylor, Anne Hunter, Gretchen Taylor, the rest of the "Taylor clan" in Minnesota, John Holmes, Dennis Evans, Lisa Nilsson, and Arlynn "Curt" Curtis, Rebecca Porter, and Joe Dillon. Your inquiries, encouragement, and advice remain truly appreciated.

This is my first book. I am now aware of how much an author owes to a competent editor; I was fortunate enough to have two good people in my corner. Thank you, Sarah Morrison and Jennifer Robins, for your patience, encouragement, and sound advice as this book progressed through the various stages of publishing.

Finally, I am truly indebted to all of the teachers I have had, from all walks of life, who challenged, encouraged, dared, cajoled, forced, invited, and inspired me to never stop asking questions. You were aware of liberal education's gift: that only the big questions have the possibility of saving us from becoming small people. Thank you for your efforts to pass this gift along.

Introduction

This text is ultimately a guidebook. When we travel through a country that is new to us, we have to pay close attention to the terrain and the landmarks. Intellectual travels are much the same. Because you are a guide for others who are beginning their journeys, this volume will help you point out major landmarks that characterize the landscape of Western thought. Doing so will improve your students' reading comprehension and general understanding of current intellectual debates.

The "landmarks" discussed in this volume involve many of the principal concepts underlying religion, scientific research, economic activity, ethics, government, philosophy, and other significant endeavors of an advanced society. Most of the major concepts appear to us not alone, but as contradictions. Everywhere we turn, we are confronted by oppositions such as free will vs. determinism, revelatory faith vs. reason, and liberalism vs. conservatism. Like binary stars, these dualities rotate around one another and draw us into their orbits. People have grappled with these clashing concepts for thousands of years, and their struggles have carved out a path for others to follow through the intellectual thickets.

It is not possible to say whether these pervasive opposing topics in intellectual history have always been there, awaiting discovery, or whether they are merely creations of the human mind. They are as eternal as they are impossible to reconcile. Students will benefit from struggling with these contradictions. In doing so, they will be introduced to ideas that both inspired and burdened some of our greatest thinkers.

This book does not attempt to offer any resolutions to the oppositions it presents. Perhaps there are no answers to the questions posed by these important contradictions. Regardless, each generation should have the freedom, if not the obligation, to explore them. In doing so, young people will sustain the intellectual heritage of Western culture. It is hoped that they will also sharpen their minds, hone their writing skills, gain greater comprehension of what they read, and develop their abilities to engage in civil discussion. When all is said and done, perhaps these outcomes provide the greatest justification for pursuing the ideas infused in this curriculum, lending further credence to the value of the liberal arts.

How to Use This Book

This book is divided into 12 chapters. Chapter 2 provides an overview of philosophical thinking, and each of the following chapters presents an insoluble contradiction that has engaged generations of thinkers. The book routinely calls these perennial contradictions other names as well, such as "dualities," "debates," and "oppositions." Although different terms may be used, a common history applies to all of them: Each refers to a longstanding debate over important ideas in the Western intellectual tradition.

If you are interested in this book, you are most likely a professional educator. Your discretion regarding what material to use from this book is both expected and encouraged. Each chapter is written so that it can stand alone. Use this book in its entirety or parts of it as you see fit. I wrote these lessons with my gifted middle school students in mind, but they can also enrich language arts, social studies, philosophy, math, and psychology classes. High school students will also benefit from these lessons—particularly if you wish to explore a certain topic in depth or create a cross-curricular unit. Some of the chapters address sensitive topics (e.g., religion, ethnicity), so you will need to judge the maturity and ability of your students and adapt the material accordingly.

Beginning with Chapter 3, each chapter of this book uses the following format:

- ⚙ **Introduction:** This section is written for teachers, primarily to provide overall objectives, background information, and additional materials for lesson planning. However, you may choose to have gifted and advanced students read the introductory section if you believe they will benefit from its ideas.

- ⚙ **Classroom Activities and Assessments:** This section contains a variety of reproducible activities you may use to teach the material and evaluate comprehension. Materials range from scripts used to stimulate student discussion to lesson plans, quizzes, and student assignments. A guide to these classroom activities appears after each chapter's introduction.

- ⚙ **Evaluation Criteria:** In each chapter, you will find some combination of reproducible grading criteria, rubrics, and quizzes. Although suggested criteria and rubrics are provided where possible, many of the activities require subjective grading. Some of the included rubrics are fairly general, and this is by design, given the wide range of classrooms in which these materials can be used. It may be useful for you to use the rubrics and grading guidelines as a jumping off point, either modifying them or creating your own.

It is very important to point out that the classroom activities and other pedagogical materials in this book are not meant to be comprehensive. Each chapter skims the surface of a somewhat daunting topic, the goal being that students' interest will be sparked and their critical thinking skills engaged. Use the background information on each age-old dilemma as a foundation for any lesson or discussion you choose to design. I hope the materials provided will help you in this endeavor.

Keeping a Discussion Alive: Some Suggestions From the Trenches

Most of the curricular materials in this book are designed to stimulate discussion. My students prefer to read scripts aloud in class, which often fosters discussion before the script is even finished. Other activities may also encourage classroom discussion, especially if students are asked to share what they have written for journal entries or assignments.

If possible, control the size of the group.

You may be able to have a classroom discussion with up to 15 students, but this number is the "tipping point" between conversation and chaos. If you have a large class (as most will), you may need to number students off and break them into discussion groups of approximately 4–6 students. You may then wrap up the discussion with comments from each group. Use the **Discussion Evaluation** slip (p. 10) to evaluate student discussions.

Lay out some ground rules before any discussion begins.

It is best to have a very simple list of 3–4 expectations for group discussions posted in the room. Better yet, post a list of the evaluative criteria on the Discussion Evaluation slip. These are excellent discussion expectations for any size group.

Students may need to be taught how to have a discussion.

Unfortunately, for many students, discussion at home is rare and punctuated by noise from a television. Also, texting while among friends has become the norm, and thus students are often conditioned to attend to communication devices instead of people. There are many resources for how to teach discussion skills. Don't get overwhelmed; students mainly need practice and feedback about how they are doing.

Do not push an agenda in a discussion.

Too often, discussions led by teachers, parents, and other adults are simply vehicles for hidden curricula (actually fairly obvious curricula). Students learn how to say "the right thing" for credit, but they do not learn how to think for themselves.

Do not try to reach a conclusion or right answer.

For philosophical discussions such as those in this book, attempting to reach a definite conclusion will ultimately suppress discussion. Instead, use active listening techniques. Quickly summarize a student's comments and ask questions that will allow him or her to clarify terms, examine assumptions, and evaluate the implications of his or her statements.

Be Socrates!

Listen carefully, summarize the student's statement quickly and accurately, and then ask additional questions. You can use some standard "starters" for your questions, such as the following:

- What I hear you saying is . . .

- What thoughts led you to this conclusion?

- *(Student's name)* says that *(repeat or rephrase student's point)*. Who agrees with this?

- I hear you saying *(summarize student's point)*. Does anyone have a different opinion?

- If what you are saying is true, then what should we do in the future?

- If what you are saying is true, then why do other people have different opinions? What might you tell those people?

- What kinds of people might be most likely to agree or disagree with you? Why?

Use writing as a tool to improve the discussion's content.

You may want to try one of the following tactics:

1. Pose an open-ended question as a prompt, and have students write a response before they can speak. When you call on them, ask them to read what they have written.

2. Do the same as above, only instead of having students write individual responses, ask groups of 4–5 students to write comments or reactions to each other's responses. This activity may take some practice and prior instruction from the teacher so that students know how to react to one another appropriately and adequately.

3. Have students write responses to a question on note cards. Collect them and shuffle the deck before reading them aloud. You can instruct students to write their names on the cards, or leave them anonymous.

4. Assign students a question for the next day. Tell them that you will collect their written answers (as part of an assignment) prior to discussion.

5. Assign creative writing as a discussion prompt. Students may write R.A.F.T.s (wherein they are given a role, an audience, a format, and a topic; see Culham, 2003), letters to particular historical or fictional

characters (e.g., Jane Goodall, Don Quixote), original dialogues, and so on. Some ideas are included at the end of each chapter.

6. Have students come up with their own questions. Students may take turns assigning questions to peers in their groups or to the whole class. It is important to teach students about the structure and importance of open-ended questions before assigning this task. Too often, they will choose questions requiring simple yes or no responses, or questions that require only rote recall rather than careful thought.

7. Have students create a formal résumé for a famous individual (e.g., Galileo) or list what they would put on a Facebook page for the person.

8. Assign persuasive speeches, editorials, advertisements, public service announcements, billboards, bumper sticker slogans, T-shirt messages, and other genres of written communication. All of these exercises can foster lively discussion, as students will relish the chance to be creative.

Manage the flow of discussion.

It is helpful to distribute popsicle sticks or other easily manipulated items as "tickets" to talk. Once a student uses all of his or her tickets, that student relinquishes the right to say anything more. This prevents any one student from dominating the discussion.

Monitor small groups.

Have students trade off playing the role of facilitator for group discussions. For older students—particularly gifted and advanced students—the structure of assigning rigid group roles rarely works well. Generally, only the facilitator role can be assigned; students do not usually accept other manufactured roles, such as secretary or timekeeper, as they seem arbitrary.

Have students move around the room.

If opinions begin to diverge, move students with similar opinions to one side of the room, and move those with another opinion to the opposite side of the room. Those students who are "on the fence" can remain in the middle. Both sides then try to convince those sitting in the middle to join them by using persuasive arguments. You may also assign discussion groups based on which students agree with one another. After the students write and talk, schedule a debate between the groups.

Thinking Philosophically

Objectives

- ⚙ Students will describe the types of questions and lines of thinking that may be explored in philosophy.

- ⚙ Students will evaluate the purpose of philosophy.

Each topic in this book is rooted in some branch of philosophical inquiry. The introductory lesson included in this chapter is designed to help students develop their own working definitions of philosophical thought. Students are often hampered by either a fairly stereotypical understanding of philosophical dialogue, or by a narrow view of philosophy. For instance, when asked about philosophy, they will frequently parrot trite questions such as, "What is the meaning of life?" Likewise, they need assistance in understanding that the concepts explored in the current curriculum are largely philosophical in nature.

If they understand philosophy at all, students often think that it is for university professors, bearded Greek men in togas, or college students in coffee houses. The goal is to help students understand that philosophical dialogue is accessible to—and important for—all of us.

Introduction to Philosophy Lesson

1. Define what *philosophy* means. The term comes from the Greek word *philosophos*. It combines *philos*, meaning beloved or loving, and *sophos*, meaning wise. The term sophos is derived from Sophia, a goddess of wisdom for the Gnostics, a widespread group of religious believers who lived during the time of Jesus and for decades afterward. Many were Christians, but they were largely driven out by early Christian leaders and became forgotten. The word *gnostic* comes from the Greek *gnosis*, meaning knowledge. A few modern derivatives of this term are *diagnosis*, *prognosis*, and *agnostic*.

2. Explain that philosophy involves asking deep and challenging questions. Have students arrange the following questions along a continuum, with the most probing questions at one end, and the most superficial questions at the other. They should represent the questions on a picture of a beach leading from sand (where they should put shallower questions) to water that gets deeper and deeper (for more probing questions).

   ⊙ Who?
   ⊙ What?
   ⊙ Where?
   ⊙ Why?
   ⊙ When?
   ⊙ How?

3. Circulate and look at students' drawings. Ask students to clarify why they arranged their continuums the way they did. Encourage them to ask others about their answers or to persuade others to change their responses. Generally, the "How?" and "Why?" questions are thought to be the deepest.

4. Encourage students to explore the question of "Why?" Ask students why they think this is the deepest or most probing question. Repeatedly asking why things happen or exist leads us to question our assumptions and to get at the very foundations of our thinking.

5. Briefly introduce Socrates (many biographies are available online). After sharing enough of his story to help students understand his mission, share the following quote, attributed to Socrates: "The

unexamined life is not worth living." Ask students to write one-paragraph responses to one or all of the following questions:

- ⊙ What did Socrates mean when he said this?
- ⊙ Do you agree with him?
- ⊙ Are there people who would prefer not to examine life or ask difficult questions?

Students' responses to these questions are often interesting. Adolescents are particularly astute about those authority figures who do not want them asking troubling questions. The importance of independent thinking resonates with this age group.

6. Conclude with a general statement about how exploring the age-old dilemmas in Western thought forces us to explore our basic assumptions and to ask critical questions.

Discussion and Assessment

Use the **Discussion Evaluation** slip provided on page 10. Once your class becomes familiar with the criteria, you may simply wish to use a blank spreadsheet and tell students that they will begin with 16 points (or however many points you choose). Share the criteria with them, and indicate that if they do not meet a given criterion, such as "listens respectfully," then points will be deducted. Make sure that all students understand the criteria and that you have provided examples of appropriate behavior.

In my own classroom, I am often more concerned about listening than I am about talking. Most of my students are quite verbal. There are some who prefer simply to listen. As long as they do so attentively and demonstrate comprehension of the material in their written work, I will give them full credit in the category of "offered relevant questions and comments." It is up to you, of course, how to define these terms and parameters for your students.

In most of the chapters of this book, questions designed to serve as journal prompts or discussion questions are presented after essays and scripted dialogues. When evaluating journal responses, I try to focus on student ideas and evidence of comprehension, not mechanics, so that students concentrate on their critical thinking rather than on more minute issues. I always award points for ideas that are supported with evidence from the reading material, as well as giving points for strong reasoning.

Discussion Evaluation

Topic(s) Discussed

_____

_____

_____

**Four points are possible for each item below
(16 possible points).**

Before Discussion

Prepared for discussion (completed readings, journal reflections, and
other materials): _____

During Discussion

Offered relevant questions and comments: _____

Listened respectfully: _____

Spoke appropriately and respectfully: _____

Total Points _____

Make Up Your Mind © Prufrock Press

Discussion Evaluation

Topic(s) Discussed

_____

_____

_____

**Four points are possible for each item below
(16 possible points).**

Before Discussion

Prepared for discussion (completed readings, journal reflections, and
other materials): _____

During Discussion

Offered relevant questions and comments: _____

Listened respectfully: _____

Spoke appropriately and respectfully: _____

Total Points _____

Make Up Your Mind © Prufrock Press

CHAPTER

3

Nature vs. Nurture

Objectives

⚙ Students will explore how genetics and environment combine to produce a variety of conditions and behaviors.

⚙ Students will recognize the contribution of the dynamic opposition of nature and nurture to intellectual debate.

⚙ Students will be able to contrast necessary and sufficient causes and apply these concepts to the nature vs. nurture debate.

⚙ Students will evaluate how research concerning the nature vs. nurture debate is designed, as well as the explanatory power of that research.

Introduction

The nature vs. nurture opposition has other names, such as *genes vs. environment* and *heredity vs. upbringing*. In all cases, though, the terms we use refer to comparing the traits we are born with to those we acquire through experience.

Some aspects of the nature vs. nurture construct are rarely disputed. For example, nobody regards the claim that most people are born with thumbs as particularly controversial. Our thumbs are genetically programmed and obviously inherited from our thumb-bearing predecessors. In contrast, it is often debated whether men are more physically aggressive than woman because of inherited traits, or as a result of their upbringing. Topics like this make the clash between nature and nurture much more contentious and significant.

Debate also rages over whether—and to what degree—biological disorders such as autism and schizophrenia are inherited or acquired (Rutter, 2006). Similar debates over IQ rise to national attention at fairly regular intervals, often accompanied by media hype. Finally, there are many less controversial but very interesting articles and discussions focusing on personality traits and the degree to which they are inherited, as opposed to being formed by environment (Bouchard, 1999).

How did the debate get started? There is little doubt that people have long been aware of the influence of environment and inherited traits. (It would be impossible, for instance, to domesticate animals without this knowledge.) However, the controversy over this issue has roots that extend back to Plato.

Plato proposed that the reason we are capable of knowing about the world is that we possess an innate capacity to understand universal, eternal, and nonmaterial truths from local, transitory, and material phenomena. This is illustrated by our seemingly natural ability to understand mathematical principles without having any prior experience with them (Sahakian, 1968). When combined with Christian doctrine concerning the inherently sinful nature of humans, arguments for faith in God, and other theological constructs, the powerful idea of an inborn human nature became generally accepted (Stumpf, 1983). René Descartes, who exerted immense influence on the history of thought, assumed that we were born with certain innate dispositions that allowed us to reason towards truth. Like Plato, he found mathematics to be a remarkable example of inherent mental capacities. Because of this, Descartes tried to create a philosophical system that would have the methodological rigor, clarity, and certainty of mathematics (Stumpf, 1983). Indeed, mathematics does seem to pose mysterious questions about how the mind can understand and reason with immaterial symbols and concepts independent of experience.

The assumption of innate knowledge was overturned in the 17th century when John Locke, a British philosopher, elevated the role of experience in establishing knowledge. He introduced the concept (radical for

his time) that the mind at birth is a *tabula rasa* (blank tablet) "void of all characters, without any ideas" (Locke, 1690/1976, p. 171). He proposed that sensations gleaned from our environment, combined with our reflections on these sensations, form the foundation of thought. Although he did not debate using the terms nature and nurture, Locke would have voted on the side of nurture (for the most part).

The nature vs. nurture debate may have been cradled in the lap of philosophy, but it was kidnapped and reared by science. The contributions of Charles Darwin and modern geneticists beginning with Gregor Mendel paved the way to a greater understanding of the mechanisms of nature. A number of biologists, ethnologists, geneticists, primatologists, and psychologists have made it possible, over time, for us to consider human behavior from the vantage point of natural selection. The burgeoning fields of neurology, biology, and experimental psychology have also contributed to the nature vs. nurture debate. Investigators have documented and experimented with instincts, reflexes, brain scans, cognition, learned behaviors, and the mysteries of sensation and perception.

Finally, sociologists, educators, therapists, anthropologists, and others in both theoretical and applied social sciences have offered their own insights into humans and their environments. Many have studied ways in which social problems could be ameliorated by environmental changes.

Today, the popular debate over innate characteristics and environmental experience has little to with epistemology and much more to do with the intersection of psychology and social policy. We do not wring our hands, as Plato may have, over how we manage to grasp the classification of triangles. Instead, modern people are more concerned about human capacities, social inequalities, and deep-seated behaviors. We are both troubled by and curious about how much of our intelligence we may inherit from our parents. We want to know whether buying toy guns for children will make them violent adults. We want to know whether education can reverse the effects of childhood deprivation and make people more productive and happy.

Contrary to what you may read in popular media sources, responsible scientists rarely claim that complex human traits, especially behavioral ones, can be attributed entirely to either nature or nurture (Rutter, 2006). A journalist once asked the famous neuropsychologist Donald O. Hebb whether nature or nurture contributed more to personality. Hebb returned fire by asking, "Which contributes more to the area of a rectangle, its length or its width?" Hebb understood that nature and nurture are inextricably bound up in determining personality.

Indeed, the dispute is no longer about nature *or* nurture; it is about nature *and* nurture—and about which domain has the greater explanatory power in any specific situation. Often, the outcome of a debate will hinge on research methods and the validity or applicability of investigative results.

Quantitative genetics (Rutter, 2006) is one fruitful area of scientific research that attempts to determine the differing effects of genetics and environmental factors on particular traits. Specifically, these researchers focus on the *variance* of a trait—for example, weight—and how much of this variance can be attributed to either genetic or environmental influences.

The common understanding of genetic variables is often oversimplified and erroneous. When talking about a particular human trait or characteristic, people will say, "There's a gene for that." This mistakenly implies that the gene directly causes the condition.

Michael Rutter, an epidemiologic researcher in pediatric psychiatry, explained in his 2006 book *Genes and Behavior: Nature-Nurture Interplay Explained* that it is generally wrong to assume that a genetic link to a disorder—depression, for instance—actually *causes* that disorder. The same holds true for more positively viewed traits, such as intelligence. Instead, it is important to realize that for complex disorders and traits, there are a host of causes, some genetic and some environmental. Furthermore, the causes themselves must be classified according to whether they are merely *necessary* for the trait to be expressed, or whether they are *sufficient causes* (i.e., they cause the behavior, disorder, or trait to be observed).

For example, think about starting a car. We may assume that starting the car relies merely upon turning the ignition key. (We might think that turning the key is a sufficient cause.) However, for this to work, a wide array of other necessary causes must be present. Your car must have a battery, it must have functioning wires, there must be gas in the tank, the alternator must be operational, and so forth. Turning the ignition key may start the car, but this on switch depends upon the complicated interaction of many variables.

The same dynamic interplay of necessary and sufficient causes affects nature and nurture as they influence human traits. As a result, there are sometimes many paths to one resulting trait or behavior. To illustrate this point, Rutter (2006) cited five separate paths to clinical depression. These causes varied from genetic codes for neurotransmitter production to stressful events in a person's life. Thus, the *combination* of nature and nurture is what activates the gene for depression.

Another fruitful area of research is the study of twins. Identical twins who are adopted and reared apart provide an ideal experimental design. This way, we have two genetically identical humans reared in different environments. Obviously, shared traits could be assumed to be genetic, and differing traits could then be assumed to be the result of environment.

In a study of three collections of data for monozygotic (identical) twins, Bouchard (1999) found that just over 40% of the variance in personality traits (neuroticism, extraversion, agreeableness, conscientiousness, and openness) could be attributed to genetics. These data are powerful; however, it is also critical to note the potential influence of environmental factors.

Recent and future advances in genetics (e.g., the mapping of the human genome) may produce a far more nuanced understanding of the dynamic interplay between nature and nurture. On the other hand, it is possible that the nurture side of the equation will continue to shrink. Regardless, scientists whose research crosses the divide between nature and nurture are eager to point out that both variables shape us. Furthermore, it appears to be our "nature" to constantly shape our environment; in the near future, this may well include genetic modification. The domains of nature and nurture will only entwine further, like the labyrinthine strands of a Celtic knot.

Classroom Activities and Assessments

Nature vs. Nurture: An Analogy and Discussion Lesson (pp. 17–19) is a guided discussion that provides students with a conceptual framework for the nature vs. nurture debate. **Nature *and* Nurture** (pp. 20–23) is a challenging article for students to read. The article contains critical vocabulary terms and introduces students to the distinction between necessary and sufficient causes. It is followed by a **quiz** (pp. 24–25; answer key on p. 34) that will assess student comprehension and critical thinking about the subject matter. **Analogy of the Stream: A Lesson on Multiple Pathways to One Condition** (pp. 26–28) is a lesson utilizing imagery to help students understand the complex ways in which nature and nurture combine to create conditions such as depression. **We've Got Chemistry, Baby!** (pp. 29–30) is a short article about the biochemical basis of love. You can either read it aloud to students and discuss the questions, or you can have students read the article and either discuss the questions in groups or respond to them in writing. (The article also lends itself well to discussions about free will vs. determinism, the subject of Chapter 8.) **Dear Dr. Nature and Dr. Nurture** (p. 31; grading standards on p. 35) is an assignment requiring students to assume the role of an expert and respond to a phobia-related question from both the nature and the nurture perspectives. **Investigation Poster: Topics in the Nature vs. Nurture Debate** (p. 32; grading criteria on p. 36) is an assignment allowing students to explore one of the many controversial and perplexing issues emanating from the nature vs. nurture debate. Students will create an investigative report and poster on a chosen topic (suggested topics are offered), which may be presented in class. Finally, for **Thinking About Science** (p. 33; answer key on p. 37), students will need to be familiar with the general purpose of scientific research and the effect of experimental design. The assignment can be individually assigned, used for enrichment, or used as a structure for a lesson on research design.

Nature vs. Nurture: An Analogy and Discussion Lesson

Materials

If you wish, you can bring in an apple and an onion. If not, just draw these on the blackboard or display images.

Objective

Students will understand the differences between nature and nurture, based on an analogy, and they will contemplate the implications of these differences.

Procedure

1. Draw or display an apple and an onion. Ask students to imagine cutting down the center of the apple. Have them draw what the apple would look like. Ask them to do the same for the onion.

2. If you like, you can have students volunteer to share their images.

3. Explain that apples have very well-defined cores, whereas onions contain successive layers, with nothing different in their centers.

4. Write "nature" under the apple picture and "nurture" under the onion picture. (If you are using a real apple and a real onion, simply improvise with index cards or another method.)

5. Ask students the questions listed below. Have them respond on scratch paper or in journals before speaking. This allows them to reflect and gives everyone a chance to think about the analogy, making connections on an individual level.

Questions

1. **Why would an apple be labeled "nature" and an onion be labeled "nurture"?** (Lead students towards the conclusion that nature theories assume that we have a "core" that influences who we are and how we behave. Conversely, the successive layers of the onion illustrate "layers" of experience. There is no core, only deepening layers.)

2. **Depression is condition that affects millions of people. Some of the symptoms are feelings of hopelessness, a loss of joy in life, irritability, and persistent feelings of worthlessness. To**

what extent do you think depression is caused by our environments? To what extent do you think it is caused by our genes?
(After discussing these questions, share the following information. According to twin studies [Rutter, 2006], about 37% of the
variance in the population of depressed people is due to genetics.
The rest is likely caused by environmental factors [as well as some
measurement error]. Other studies put this estimate at closer to
70%. Although the genetic factor is large, it seems that what characterizes most depressed individuals is a genetic susceptibility to
depression that is then triggered by environmental events. So in
this case, the condition is caused both by the genetic core and by
the experiential layers at work. As with most complex phenomena
such as depression, humans appear to be onions with cores—or
apples with layers.)

3. **Does anyone in your family have a genetic tendency towards a
health problem, like diabetes or heart disease? Is it possible to
control these problems?**

4. **Does anyone say that you act like a parent, grandparent, or other
relative? Knowing what you know at this point, do you think
they are right? Is it possible to control this trait or condition?**
(This discussion could go in a variety of directions. With some
luck and prodding, students may realize that certain inherited
tendencies or conditions, such as diabetes, are easier to treat or
control than others.) **How would we control being a worrywart
like Aunt Edna, or a daredevil like dashing Uncle Derrick?**
(Students should be led to observe the rich interplay between a
tendency and what can be controlled in the environment.)

5. **Bacteria are exact copies of their parents. We are not—animals
like us take half of their genes from their mothers and half
from their fathers. What are the potential advantages of this?**
(Encourage students to consider how this helps us adapt; we are
more flexible because either the mother's or the father's side may
have the better genes for a particular challenge, such as famine,
climate change, or disease.)

6. **Also, bacteria don't learn much. They behave in a very programmed way—their actions are inflexible, strictly programmed by nature. We do not exhibit many highly programmed behaviors, and neither do other mammals with a
high degree of intelligence. What could the advantages be of
having a brain that can flexibly respond to nurture?** (Guide stu-

dents to discuss how, with nurture, knowledge and technology can be passed down from generation to generation and can be recorded, helping advance a species.)

Nature *and* Nurture

Read the following article, paying close attention to the words in bold.

Imagine an apple and an onion on a cutting board. You turn the apple on its side, slice vertically through the center, and find a core running the length of the apple. Now imagine doing the same with the onion. Unlike the apple, the onion has no real core—only nested layers that look like concentric rings.

The differences between an apple and an onion are **analogous** to the differences between theories about our traits. Those who believe that our **traits**, such as musical talent, are strictly the result of our genetics would state that we have cores, like apples. They would claim that our genetic cores dictate our temperaments, unique talents, levels of intelligence, and general health. For such theorists, *nature*—in the form of our chromosomes—provides an **ineluctable** blueprint that dictates everything about us.

Those who believe, on the other hand, that our traits are caused solely by environmental influences would assert that we have no core that controls everything. Instead, we are the products of **successive** layers of experience. It is how we are *nurtured* along the way that dictates the most about us.

In reality, people who study genetics and environment are not usually strictly "apple theorists" or "onion theorists." Almost all psychologists, geneticists, biologists, and other knowledgeable people readily accept that we are products of both nature and nurture. So we are really onions with cores. The debate is not over what causes us to be a certain way, but over how *much* of a trait (musical ability, for instance) is genetic, as opposed to environmental. Much research is done in this area.

The research and debate concerning whether genetics dominates environment or vice versa are sometimes complicated. In some cases, the evidence is obvious. For example, if you are like most people, then you have lungs instead of gills (a safe bet). Nobody is going to claim that you developed lungs as the result of environmental influences. You were simply genetically programmed to have lungs.

Now suppose that you are a coal miner who has developed pneumoconiosis, commonly referred to as "black lung disease." Clearly, you were not born with black lung disease; it was acquired from your environment (nurture). Nobody would claim that you were completely genetically programmed for black lung disease. You had to come into contact with coal dust to get it.

If only the debate could be as simple as these examples! Things become much more complex when we consider schizophrenia, intelligence, ADHD, antisocial behavior, colon cancer, musical ability, hypertension, extraversion, and a host of other human characteristics and ailments.

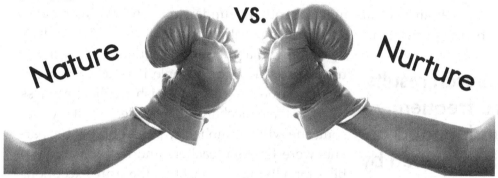

Scientists who study the **interaction** of nature and nurture have to use special research designs (in other words, they have to structure their research projects in certain ways) and tools to determine how much each factor (nature or nurture) contributes to a particular trait. Once they determine how much of a trait is explained by genetics, they then assume that the rest is explained by environment and errors in measuring during the study.

The term these scientists often use is **heritability**. This term has a very specific meaning and is often misunderstood. The term refers to a proportion, usually a percentage, of a given population of people. If a scientist says that the heritability of antisocial behavior is 41%, that is *not* saying that 41% of any bully's behavior is the result of genetics. Instead, the scientist is saying that 41% of the variance of this trait, measured in a *particular group of people,* is due to genetics. Variance is the range of behavior—so here, from never engaging in antisocial behavior through exhibiting the most antisocial behavior.

It helps to understand, in a simplified format, what steps scientists take to arrive at an estimate of heritability. Scientists start by identifying the group to be studied, and then they measure the presence, absence, or degree of a certain trait. Finally, they do the research to separate out the causes (genes or environment). After that is done, they can give an estimate of the proportion of causes that are probably genetic. As always, the findings are more valid when applied only to the group being studied (e.g., fourth graders with learning disabilities), and less valid when applied to a very different group (e.g., adults with learning disabilities).

It is very important to point out how wrong it is to make a prediction about any individual in a group based on overall group data. Saying that 41% of the variance of antisocial behavior in a research sample is due to genetics may be correct. However, saying that Joe, a member of this group, is "41% likely" to be antisocial would be wrong. You cannot make a totally accurate prediction about an individual based on group data.

Research results are frequently misunderstood and misinterpreted by the public. Some people relish pointing out how "wrong" a study is by claiming that they are exceptions to the general results of a study. For example, if a study points out that children raised by English teachers are less likely to have mechanical aptitude, it is likely that someone will triumphantly point out that his parents were English teachers and he fixes automobiles for a living. The fact that there are exceptions to a study's findings does not mean that its results aren't correct in most cases. (In this example, this would simply mean that although some English teachers do have children who grow up to have mechanical aptitude, English teachers' children are still *less likely* than children in the general population are to grow up to be mechanically minded.)

> **Research results are frequently misunderstood and misinterpreted by the public.**

Naturally, the best studies are the ones with airtight designs. Twin studies are extremely important in this field, because researchers can study identical twins who have been raised in different homes. Because identical twins have *exactly* the same genes, any difference between twins is very likely to be the result of the environment.

As if all of this were not confusing enough, scientists must also classify causes of a particular trait or condition. There are two general categories of causes—**necessary** and **sufficient**. Necessary causes are the factors that must be present in order for a certain result to occur. Sufficient causes are the factors (or the factor) that actually create the result.

Let's use the example of a forest fire, something a bit simpler than genetics, to illustrate these terms. The necessary causes of a forest fire are factors that must be present for a forest fire to occur, such as drought, lots of dead timber, hot weather, and plenty of easily ignitable material, like pine needles or leaves. None of these, however, will automatically create a fire. You need a sufficient cause to serve as the spark for the event to occur—for instance, lightning or an unattended campfire.

For a few human conditions, it is simple to determine which causes are sufficient and which are necessary, and to divide these neatly between genes and environment. Lactose intolerance is a good example. It has a necessary cause that is genetic (the physical inability to produce lactase, an enzyme that helps digest the lactose found in dairy products), and it has a sufficient cause that is environmental (drinking milk, for instance). The treatment for this condition is easy—just avoid dairy products, the sufficient cause.

Unfortunately, most research into human problems and conditions yields much more complicated results. Unlike with lactose intolerance, where the necessary cause is genetic and the sufficient cause is environmental, many conditions and traits have necessary and sufficient causes in both domains. In other words, there are necessary and sufficient causes in the environment *and* in the genes. Depression, for instance, can be caused and triggered by a wide variety of factors, such as genetics, other physical disorders that are either genetic or acquired, and environmental factors, such as the loss of a job.

In spite of these complications, the research on genetics and environment must continue. This research may help us find ways to prevent and cure many diseases. It may also help us determine how best to parent or educate people with particular risk factors or with complex conditions such as autism and schizophrenia. With the advent of the fully mapped human genome, it has become possible to conduct even more powerful research into the fantastically complex interaction of nature and nurture.

Nature *and* Nurture:
Thinking and Comprehension Quiz

Circle the best response.

1. What would be the best alternate title for this article?

    a) "Necessary and Sufficient Causes"
    b) "How Much Onion and How Much Core?"
    c) "Understanding Research About Nurture"
    d) "Problems With Genetic Research"

2. Why would a scientist have to be careful about concluding that a certain trait is caused by a particular set of genes?

    a) The scientist would need to know whether environment also plays a part in the trait.
    b) The scientist would need to know whether other genes might also contribute to the trait.
    c) The scientist would need to know if the trait were present in people who lacked that set of genes.
    d) All of the above are true.

3. Which of the following is **not** a necessary cause of heart problems?

    a) A history of heart disease in the person's family
    b) Overstressing the heart while playing basketball
    c) A diet rich in fatty foods
    d) Lack of exercise

4. The term *heritability* means . . .

    a) The proportion of a person's behavior that is determined by genetics.
    b) The proportion of total genes causing someone to have a group trait.
    c) The proportion of a trait's variance within a group that is determined by genetics.
    d) The proportion of variation within a group's genetics.

5. What makes identical twin studies so important?

    a) Differences between twins are more likely due to environment.
    b) Most identical twins have been raised in separate environments.
    c) Identical twins are genetically the same.
    d) Answers a and c are true.

6. If a friend told you, "Researchers found a gene that causes 80% of criminal behavior," how might you explain the dangers of making conclusions from this research? Write a one-paragraph answer.

_____

_____

_____

_____

_____

_____

_____

_____

_____

_____

_____

_____

_____

_____

_____

_____

_____

Analogy of the Stream: A Lesson on Multiple Pathways to One Condition

Introduction

Researchers have noted multiple pathways to depression. Some of them involve genetic or biological risk factors. For instance, some people may not produce enough of the neurotransmitter serotonin. Others may have a disorder that causes fatigue or pain, such as acute arthritis, and this disorder reduces the person's production of serotonin over time.

Likewise, there are multiple causes of depression after conception. Some of these are the consequences of life experience. A person may go through a divorce, go to war, lose a job, become addicted to alcohol, become seriously injured, flunk out of college, or simply develop poor coping skills over time. These causes can occur alone or in combination, and each puts a person at risk for depression. With this lesson, you will impart to students the concept of "multiple genetic and environmental paths" to one trait—in this case, depression.

Materials

For this lesson, you'll need a chalkboard, whiteboard, or interactive blackboard, as well as markers or other writing tools.

Objective

Students will be able to explain how genetic and environmental causes can combine to produce multiple pathways leading to the same trait or condition.

Procedure

1. Before the lesson, draw a wide stream running horizontally across the board, with an island in the center. Label the island "Birth." Draw a stick figure (if you are artistically inclined, feel free to put in more effort) on the lower shore. On the upper shore, write "Depression." In the middle of the two stream channels, scattered about, draw several stones. Some can be large, some smaller, some close, and some widely scattered.

2. Begin by asking students how many of them have ever stepped on exposed stones to cross a stream or river. Discuss the fact that

some stones form a direct path, some can be skipped over, and some may be so scattered that you reach the other shore far away from the spot you intended.

3. Draw students' attention to the board. Point to the stick figure and tell students that this person is going to become depressed. Briefly explain what depression is, including symptoms, duration, and other relevant information. You may want to point out that millions of American adults live with a mood disorder, mostly depression. Explain that this illustration and analogy will help them understand the concept of multiple pathways.

4. Draw a path across two stones leading to "Birth." Label these stones "low serotonin" and "parents struggled with depression." Then point out that the person took a path involving these two causes.

5. Draw the stick person on the island. Now label some stones and draw a path across them to the "Depression" side of the stream. You might label these stones "has car accident," "hates job," "doesn't exercise," and so forth. Point out that the stick person had all of these things happen on the path in addition to having the previous genetic risk factors for depression before birth. Ask students how likely they think it is that this person will become depressed.

6. Draw another stick person. Have this person skip all the way to "Birth" without touching a risk-factor stone. Then have this person hit several stones on the other side of the "Birth" island. Have this person hit only one stone that the first stick person hit—they have one risk factor in common. Other risk factors may include "got a divorce," "fought in Afghanistan," "flunked out of college," "lives in a rainy climate," and so forth. Show that for this person, to become depressed involved only environmental (nongenetic) factors.

7. You may want to continue labeling rocks and demonstrating different pathways to depression. The point will become clear to students, who may contribute ideas as to how depression could be developed or avoided.

Assessment

Have students do a 3-minute "quick write" in which they write a paragraph that explains the main point of the analogy and how it illustrates multiple paths towards one condition. You can either collect these, have students share them, or circulate and check some or all of them.

Questions

1. Can you imagine another trait or condition that might have multiple pathways?

2. Can you think of a positive trait—such as being a talented guitarist or snowboarder—that a person could have via multiple pathways?

3. How could multiple pathways make research difficult?

4. Running long distances helps people deal with depression, because running causes our bodies to produce endorphins, chemicals in the brain that make us feel better. If a person runs too hard, gets injured, and then gets depressed, was this depression caused by genetic or environmental factors?

We've Got Chemistry, Baby!

Perhaps you have heard someone say that two actors in a romantic comedy had "chemistry." This is an interesting choice of words, because when it comes to romance, there may be more chemistry involved than we care to admit.

Where lovebirds are concerned, there are two important types of chemical substances: hormones and neurotransmitters. **Hormones** are chemicals produced by our bodies. They help regulate how the body functions, and they can affect everything from digestion and emotions to behavior. **Neurotransmitters** are chemicals in the brain that assist in the transmission of nerve impulses from one nerve cell to the next. They can also affect a wide array of bodily functions, including mood and behavior.

When people fall in love, their bodies produce both an important neurotransmitter and a critical hormone. In the beginning, during the "infatuation stage," a person's body produces large amounts of **dopamine**, a neurotransmitter that is associated with feelings of pleasure (Foreman, 2009). Intriguingly, people with substance addictions often have brains that, once addicted to a substance, need more of that substance (and often in greater amounts) in order to respond. It is possible that very flirtatious individuals are acting in part out of a craving for dopamine. Couples who stay together move beyond the infatuation stage. As the saying goes, "newlyweds learn to live together." It turns out that another chemical is responsible for couples feeling close and comfortable with one another, and it is produced from the first time two people see one another. This chemical is a hormone called **oxytocin**. Just like dopamine, oxytocin is found in many creatures. However, it is highest in creatures that *pair bond* (the term biologists—those hopeless romantics—reserve for mating for life). Oxytocin is a hormone that is responsible for feelings of warmth and caring. Mothers of newborns produce lots of it, but fathers and males in pair-bonding relationships also produce it. As a matter of fact, merely spraying oxytocin into the nostrils of test subjects in conflict situations produced more positive behavior (Foreman, 2009).

Long-term couples still produce dopamine, but oxytocin adds another ingredient to the recipe of love, making the relationship more enduring. Perhaps most interesting is that oxytocin is related to another hormone called **vasopressin**. This chemical (which has been extensively studied in prairie voles, of all creatures) seems to enhance the brain's reward circuits. Once vasopressin is released, mated pairs will feel pleasure simply by being in one another's company. Monogamous species of voles have more neural receptor sites for vasopressin than nonmonogamous rodents who "play the field" ("Gene Transfer," 2001).

What about when we first fall in love? It turns out there are quite a few chemicals involved. One interesting study conducted at the University of Chicago discovered that when presented with T-shirts that had already been worn, women (unaware that the T-shirts had been worn already) overwhelmingly preferred shirts worn by males who were genetically similar to their fathers (Gupta, 2002). There is also considerable debate about whether airborne chemicals called pheromones, which are used for mate attraction among many other animals, also work with humans (Pines, 2008). This hasn't stopped manufacturers from producing "pheromone cologne" to help us gain an edge on the competition! Time will tell whether these silent messengers are as effective as Cupid's arrow.

Although we may prefer to think that we choose our mates, it is equally possible that nature does it for us, at least in large part. Perhaps, as the biologist Richard Dawkins (2006) maintained, we really are simply a means for genes to make more genes.

Questions

1. It turns out that we may be right when we say that a couple has chemistry. Does it bother you that love might be chemical?

2. When it comes to love, is it caused by nature, nurture, or both?

3. How much control do you think we have over love?

4. Is infatuation an addiction?

Dear Dr. Nature and Dr. Nurture

For this assignment, you must assume two roles: The first is Dr. Sidney Nurture, and the second is Dr. Chris Nature. They are both respected psychologists and advice columnists, and they never agree. The good doctors are asked to respond to a problem sent in by a loyal reader. Dr. Nurture will answer first, and then Dr. Nature will write a response.

Dear Doctors,

I am going to the Bahamas for vacation, and my friend wants me to go diving with her. I want to do this, but I am deathly afraid of sharks. I know that sharks rarely pose any danger to divers, and that a person is more likely to get struck by lightning than bitten by a shark. I remember seeing a scary movie about sharks when I was a kid, but that was a long time ago. My mom tells me I should stop watching shows about sharks, but I don't watch TV shows like that very often. How did I get this fear?

Sincerely,

"Shark Bait"

Dr. Nurture's Answer:

_____

_____

_____

_____

_____

_____

Dr. Nature's Answer:

_____

_____

_____

_____

_____

_____

Investigation Poster: Topics in the Nature vs. Nurture Debate

Create a poster about any of the topics on this page. You may also choose a topic that is not listed here, provided you obtain teacher permission first.

Poster Elements and Guidelines

1. The topic and main ideas of your investigation should be clearly indicated using a title, subheadings, and the poster's overall design. Make sure to write your name on the back of the poster!

2. You should summarize the information you found. If there are clearly two or more sides of the topic, then each perspective should have its own summary and subheading. Summaries should be typed and pasted to the poster. (Do not make your summaries in huge font size—use size 18 or smaller.)

3. The poster should contain at least two photos, graphs, charts, or other visual aids, as well as captions.

4. Hand in a bibliography listing sources for your poster.

Topic	Comments
Single-gender classrooms	Proponents claim that males and females are wired differently and require different modes of instruction. Furthermore, girls and boys may behave differently in single-sex classrooms. Even if this is true, should we segregate males and females in schools?
Female underachievement in science and math	Why do girls tend to underachieve in science and math once they reach puberty?
Fears and phobias	People are more afraid of snakes, sharks, spiders, heights, and the dark than they are of cars, even though cars kill more people than any of those things. What accounts for this?
Gender and contact sports	Why do more boys than girls play contact sports? Is this nature or nurture? What does the evidence say?
Standards for male and female beauty	These standards are surprisingly universal and relate to reproductive fitness. Do we choose mates, or does mother nature?
Love	Two neurochemicals, dopamine and oxytocin, are prevalent in couples in love. Are these chemicals in control of relationships, or do people choose whom they love?
Differences in primates	We humans share most of our genes with chimps and bonobos. They seem very much like us. What don't we share?
Genetic markers vs. symptoms	Some people have the genetic code for certain disorders, yet they do not develop those disorders. What accounts for this?
Biographies of brilliant people	Biographies of scientists, authors, and artists tell us something about how environment may influence high achievers. What can we learn from these biographies?
Biographies of child prodigies	Prodigies display talents that seem to be natural or inborn. Are these prodigies simply genetically blessed?
Experts and superstars	Are experts and superstars born with talent, or do they simply work harder?
Twin studies	Identical twins provide an ideal way to compare nature and nurture. How are they used?
Personality, skills, and intelligence	Investigate traits such as perfect pitch, criminal behavior, IQ, fearfulness, friendliness, and risk taking. To what degree are these traits nurtured, and to what degree are they the result of nature? Choose one trait and examine the evidence.

Thinking About Science

What might each research design in the chart below explain about nature vs. nurture? Use extra paper if you need to.

Research design	What research may explain
Compare shared traits of identical twins raised in different homes	
Compare different traits of identical twins raised in different homes	
Compare different traits of identical twins raised in the same home	
Compare shared traits of biologically unrelated children raised in the same home	
Compare shared genetic markers (sections of genetic code correlated with a trait) of people with schizophrenia and people without it	
Compare European and Korean definitions of female beauty	
Compare change in IQ of adopted babies compared to change in IQ of babies born into their homes	
Compare size of language areas in brains of wolves, gorillas, dolphins, and humans	
Compare biographies of great male scientists and those of great female scientists	
Compare amounts of aggressive play in chimpanzees and human children	

Nature *and* Nurture: Thinking and Comprehension Quiz

Answer Key

1. b

2. d

3. b

4. c

5. d

6. **Example response:** I would tell my friend that even if scientists had identified a gene associated with criminal behavior, it wouldn't necessarily mean that the gene *caused* this behavior. Many factors would still need to be proven. The gene may be a necessary cause for criminal behavior, but that gene may also require an environmental trigger—a sufficient cause—to make someone become a criminal.

   I would tell my friend that upon close inspection, one would see that the scientists who did the study looked only at the heritability of criminal behavior. This means that they may have compared how often a certain gene was present in a group of criminals versus in a similar-sized group of noncriminals. This would not mean, however, that the gene *caused* the criminals to commit their crimes. Also, you could not use the study to predict who would commit a crime, because you cannot make predictions about individuals based on group data.

Dear Dr. Nature and Dr. Nurture

Grading Standards

It works well to grade this assignment on a 10-point scale, with five points available for the content and accuracy of each of the two responses. The assignment may also be given as a journaling prompt to check for student understanding.

The Dr. Nurture response should state that "Shark Bait" learned to be afraid of sharks from the movie and from TV specials about sharks.

The Dr. Nature response should state that human beings are instinctively afraid of predators like sharks. This fear is part of our genetics and has kept us alive for generations. Insightful students may have Dr. Nature point out that scary movies and TV programs about sharks did not invent our fear of predators; rather, they simply take advantage of our hardwired genetic fears.

Investigation Poster: Topics in the Nature vs. Nurture Debate
Grading Criteria

Poster design: The poster should be neat and consistent with the topic and related themes. The student should use color, font, illustrations, and other design elements to present the topic and ideas, and space should be used wisely.

Summaries and content: The poster should clearly and accurately explain how the topic relates to nature and nurture, as well as the implications of the research studied for the poster.

Usage and mechanics: The poster and summary material should be free of errors in spelling, capitalization, grammar, and punctuation.

Visual aids: Charts, images, and other visual aids should be appropriate for the topic and clearly and carefully presented. Visuals should be carefully attached or drawn and should take up an appropriate amount of space on the poster—they shouldn't be too crowded, but there should not be a lot of remaining white space.

Thinking About Science

Answer Key

Research design	What research may explain
Compare shared traits of identical twins raised in different homes	*Because the twins share the same genes (nature), this design explores what may be inherited, regardless of environment (nurture).*
Compare different traits of identical twins raised in different homes	*This design isolates the influences of environment (nurture), regardless of genes (nature).*
Compare different traits of identical twins raised in the same home	*This design explores how genetically and environmentally identical people may develop unique traits through individual choices.*
Compare shared traits of biologically unrelated children raised in the same home	*This design demonstrates the power of environment, as the children would not share genes.*
Compare shared genetic markers (sections of genetic code correlated with a trait) of people with schizophrenia and people without it	*This design demonstrates the degree to which genes may play a role in this type of mental illness.*
Compare European and Korean definitions of female beauty	*This design explores how much culture (vs. shared genetics as human beings) dictates our standards of beauty.*
Compare change in IQ of adopted babies compared to change in IQ of babies born into their homes	*This design provides insight into the degree to which environment influences the trait of intelligence (as measured by an IQ test). It also shows how an IQ test, and therefore definitions of intelligence, may be susceptible to environmental influences.*
Compare size of language areas in brains of wolves, gorillas, dolphins, and humans	*By comparing the proportions of the brain that these species use to communicate, this design can help us understand the unique (or shared) qualities of human language.*
Compare biographies of great male scientists and those of great female scientists	*Because women have historically been underrepresented in science careers, this study could isolate powerful environmental factors in the development of female scientists.*
Compare amounts of aggressive play in chimpanzees and human children	*This design could indicate the degree to which aggression in children is hardwired (i.e., due to ancient genetic influence).*

CHAPTER
4

Deduction vs. Induction

Objectives

- ☼ Students will analyze critical distinctions between inductive and deductive reasoning.

- ☼ Students will use knowledge of common fallacies to critique claims relying on inductive and deductive thought processes.

- ☼ Students will appreciate how induction and deduction affect the quest for valid information.

Introduction

A novice philosopher has confronted all of us at one time or another. Typically, such individuals ask clichéd questions such as, "If a tree falls in the forest and nobody is around, does it make a sound?" Or perhaps they have asked you to prove that you are not dreaming. These attempts to make you question the validity of your knowledge may be dramatic and fairly clumsy, but they do cause you to ponder some basic assumptions.

What do we know with certainty? How much confidence can we place in our thoughts and in the evidence that the world provides? History has taught us that people can be simultaneously adamantly certain and remarkably wrong about many things. For instance, in 1989, a self-styled Soviet psychic healer (say *that* five times fast) claimed he was able to stop cars and bicycles with his mental powers (Schick & Vaughn, 2008). Convinced of his rare talent, he decided to put his psychic strengths to the ultimate test by stepping in front of an oncoming train and attempting to stop it. The experiment failed, and the man was, to put it mildly, in no condition to reformulate his hypothesis.

During the medieval era, a misguided sage noted that latrine attendants appeared immune to the bubonic plague, leading doctors to recommend that people spend time inhaling the air in public bathrooms, whereas others thought that floors, hands, mouths, and nostrils should be washed with rosewater and vinegar (Tuchman, 1978). Neither one of these remedies had anything to do with the actual cause of the disease—flea-born pathogens—and the former may well have hastened infection (in addition to ruining many people's afternoons).

We do not need to rely on the examples of flattened psychics or medieval doctors to illustrate the weaknesses of speculative thought. Modern science, even since the refinement of the scientific method, offers plenty of examples of glorious mistakes. In 1903, a member of the French Academy of Sciences, Professor Rene Blondlot, announced the discovery of a curious form of radiation he called "N-rays" (Schick & Vaughn, 2008). He claimed that when present, N-rays were capable of making targeted objects in his laboratory appear brighter. He thought N-rays could be detected by the human eye and were present in certain metals, although they were blocked by lead, like other radiation. Robert Wood, an American physicist, went to France to test Blondlot's theories. Blondlot instructed Wood to follow certain procedures so he could demonstrate his experiments. Unbeknownst to the hapless Blondlot, Wood changed experimental conditions in such a way that Blondlot, even if his theories were correct, could not observe the presence of N-rays. In spite of this, Blondlot still reported the presence of the elusive N-rays. Blondlot was not deliberately lying; his expectations had influenced his observations. It took Wood's more rigorous test to show the falseness of the theory. Once Wood revealed his manipulations, N-rays were sent to the dustbin of history (Wynn & Wiggins, 2001).

As the previous examples show, the certainty of our knowledge must be tempered with a healthy skepticism. Since the time of the pre-Socratic philosophers, entire careers have been spent attempting to determine the nature and limits of human knowledge. This branch of philosophy is called *epistemology*. The term comes from the Greek term *episteme*, mean-

ing knowledge (Parry, 2007), and the suffix *ology*, which derives from the Greek word *logos*, meaning reason. The word *logic* also comes from *logos*.

For the purposes of this brief chapter, it is best to limit the discussion of epistemology and *logos* to four important concepts that may help all of us think more clearly about knowledge and our methods of acquiring it, especially when engaged in science. These four concepts are *deduction*, *induction*, *correlation*, and *causation*.

To understand deduction and induction, we need to consider the structure of an argument. In this case, an argument does not mean a heated discussion—few of these rely on formal deduction! An argument is a statement, a disputable claim that something is true or should be believed. Arguments may be clothed in technical jargon, dispassionate analysis, or emotional rhetoric, yet all arguments are built upon their own brand of DNA—premises and conclusions.

A *premise* is a claim intended to support another claim. The final claim of an argument—the main point that premises are devised to support—is the *conclusion*. If accepted, premises will naturally lead to particular conclusions. In more sophisticated arguments, premises and conclusions can be strung together to form a complex and convincing conceptual framework. Think of the wide-ranging premises and conclusions that are woven together to support a conspiracy theory or a belief in the Loch Ness Monster.

Deductive arguments are characterized by a special relationship between premises and conclusions. In a valid deductive argument, if the premises are true, then the conclusion *has to* be true (Holowchak, 2007). Consider this classic example:

> **Premise:** All men are mortal.
> **Premise:** Socrates is a man.
> **Conclusion:** Socrates is mortal.

Deductive arguments are like houses: Their strength is based on the way they are built—on their form. Accepting the truth of the premises in the argument above gives you no choice but to accept the truth of the conclusion. If deductive arguments are built in the right order, and out of the right kinds of premises, then the truth of each premise is transferred to the conclusion. Deductive arguments like this are said to be *valid*.

There is, however, a problem with valid deductive arguments. The premises don't need to be true for the argument to be valid—the validity of an argument only refers to whether the premises actually support the conclusion. In other words, it is possible to come up with a logical-sounding, valid argument, even if the premises are utter nonsense. The following is an example of such an argument:

Premise: All turtles traveled to Earth on comets.
Premise: Sid is a turtle.
Conclusion: Sid traveled to Earth on a comet.

The argument above may sound quite logical, but unless you had tremendous confidence in the interstellar migration of turtles, you would have to conclude that the argument is sheer nonsense. This is because although the structure of the argument is valid—it preserves the truth of the premises as it forms a conclusion—there is no truth to preserve. The structure makes the argument seem plausible, but it is not.

A deductive argument that is both valid (i.e., has a truth-preserving structure) and has true premises is said to be *sound*. There are several types of deductive arguments; some are valid, and others are not. Either can have conclusions that are true, but only a valid argument is capable of preserving the actual truth-value of the premises.

We may conclude this discussion by stating two defining factors of deductive arguments. First, a deductive argument, *if it has a valid structure*, is one in which the conclusion of the argument *has to be true* if the premises are true. Second, a deductive argument is intended to provide conclusive support for its conclusions (Schick & Vaughn, 2008).

Inductive arguments are less ambitious and far more modest than deductive ones. Deductive arguments barge into the conversation, command attention, and boldly announce the truth. Inductive arguments merely attempt to support their conclusions; they try to be convincing but not conclusive. A deductive argument is a bombastic general; an inductive argument is a cautious egghead. We may formally define an inductive argument as "an argument in which the premises attempt to support its conclusion strongly, though not absolutely" (Holowchak, 2007, p. 23).

An inductive argument is considered *strong* when, if you accept the premises as true, the argument gives you more reason to believe the conclusion than not to believe it. If the premises are later found to be actually true, then this argument is said to be *cogent* (Holowchak, 2007). For example, you may state that college tuition is getting more expensive, offering the premise that your tuition bills are proportionately higher than those paid by your older friends. If you later discover statistics showing that tuition is rising at a higher rate than the inflation rate, then you have solid support for the truth of your premise, making your argu-

ment cogent. Cogent inductive arguments may be accepted as truth until a better explanation comes along.

Advances in science rely upon inductive arguments. The process may start with a number of individual observations and measurements of phenomena around us. Scientists then make a general statement about these phenomena that will, hopefully, provide an explanation. This is the hypothesis. Notice that when offering a hypothesis, scientists do not attempt to provide an airtight conclusion, as one can in deductive arguments. Instead, the hypothesis is tentative, provisional, and subject to further testing. This is the basic procedure of the scientific method.

Just as milk makes for strong bones, supportive evidence makes for a strong hypothesis. As we cast about for evidence, we may look backwards and find historical examples. We may also make predictions and see if our inductive arguments (and our hypothesis) remain intact. The entire process is inductive, because we remain cautious, knowing that if any contrary evidence emerges, we must then abandon or modify our hypothesis.

Does deduction ever come into play during investigation? It does, but it often plays a special role. Deductive arguments will be predictive. If our inductive hypothesis is true, then we *deduce* that a particular event will happen or phenomenon will be observed.

For example, I may observe that the underside of my car rusts more than my cousin's car, and he lives in southern New Mexico, while I live in Minnesota. I may hypothesize that my tires kick up rain, snow, and the ice-melting salt spread by highway crews, exposing my car to corrosive elements such as water and salt that my cousin's car doesn't encounter. This largely inductive hypothesis may be supported by evidence that my neighbor's vehicles also tend to rust more on their undersides, and that body shops in Minnesota offer to put a protective coating on the undersides of cars, something that is done less frequently in New Mexico. I may then make a prediction, really just a deduction, that *if* the rain, snow, and salt of Minnesota highways rusts cars, *then* I can purchase my cousin's car and drive it in Minnesota for a few years *and it will also rust on the underside*.

We've seen how cautious induction and bold deduction work both together and independently to help us make sense of the world. It is now time to turn our attention to two types of conclusions that allow us to gain understanding and mastery of our world. However, if these conclusions are wrong—and they often are—then we may find ourselves in terrible predicaments. As Mark Twain once remarked, "It isn't what you know that will get you into trouble; it's what you know for sure that just ain't so."

In statistics, the term *correlation* refers to the degree of association between two variables. In more common language, two or more phenomena are considered to be correlated if they are associated or related to one another. For example, in 2009 the price of oil hit record highs. During that same year, local tourism increased in many states. These two items appeared to be validly correlated—and in fact, they were. High gas prices contributed to the decisions of some vacationers to travel closer to home instead of pumping gas all the way to Yellowstone or some other far-off locale. However, for reasons explained below, we need to be cautious when assuming that correlated phenomena are truly related to one another in some causal way and are not simply coincidentally associated.

Picture a man hiking on a small path in the woods. Rounding a corner, he is confronted by a snarling pit bull. The owner of this vicious dog is nowhere in sight. The man decides that the best course of action is to stay perfectly still and not turn his back to the animal. Unbeknownst to the man, a large mountain lion is now sneaking up behind him. Upon seeing the mountain lion, the pit bull yelps and dashes away to safety. Relieved that the threatening dog has run off, the man congratulates himself for keeping a cool head in the face of imminent disaster. Then the lion attacks!

This story illustrates one of the problems with assuming that there is a causal relationship between two things that are correlated. Although the man's immobility was indeed correlated with the dog's disappearance (they happened in sequence), it was only coincidentally associated with it—the immobility did not *cause* the dog to run away. Obviously, the man erroneously concluded that *he* had caused the dog's disappearance, whereas—unfortunately for the man—it was actually the mountain lion.

We must always be cautious when positing a causal relationship between two correlated variables. As many statistics instructors admonish, "Correlation does not equal causation."

We must be cautious even when invoking a causal relationship between two events that *are* legitimately correlated. In our example of the local vacationers and gas prices, high oil prices did not themselves cause travelers to take vacations closer to home. Instead, the high prices influenced consumers to make various decisions, one of which was to reduce travel miles in order to save money. The oil prices were just one of many potential variables affecting consumer decisions.

If the universe were static, there would be no need to determine what caused anything to happen. However, the universe constantly changes,

and change sends us searching for causes (Rothman & Sudarshan, 1998). The concept of causation seems very simple. We rely upon it every day, whether we are looking before we cross a street or attempting to bake cookies. We simply "know" that certain actions or events will create certain results. We also know that causes will precede effects; it would be ridiculous to insist otherwise—although Aristotle did, and some advanced formulas in physics do as well (Rothman & Sudarshan, 1998).

In many common situations, it is quite simple to isolate causes after experiencing an effect. Remembering that causes must come before effects, you merely have to rewind your memory and follow a chain of events backwards. For instance, you may open the freezer and have a frozen chicken drop painfully onto your foot. Besides gravity, the major cause here was probably placing the chicken too close to the edge of the freezer shelf.

But what about isolating causes in more complex situations? Let's say that a psychiatrist diagnoses her patient as depressed. A clinical interview reveals that the patient recently lost his job because he failed to show up for work for 2 days. The reason he failed to show up at work was that his wife left town with the neighbor and called him from Dallas to inform him that she was filing for divorce. He acknowledges that he recently got over a gambling addiction and that the financial strain was too much for his marriage. He reveals that his mother and maternal grandfather were hospitalized for depression at various points in their lives. Finally, he tells the psychiatrist that he wishes his wife would have waited until he found another job and much-needed insurance to pay for his upcoming thyroid surgery.

So what is the cause of this patient's depression? Is it genetic, is it related to hypothyroidism, does it stem from a gambling addiction, is it a reaction to stressful life events, or is it some mixture of all of these factors? As with most significant events and situations, this patient's depression has numerous and complex causes. We cannot rely on a simple, linear flow chart. This situation calls for a recipe!

Even our example of the frozen chicken falling from the freezer is more complicated that we might assume. First, if the freezer were in outer space, the chicken would not fall. We have to assume that gravity is a cause, yet Einstein taught us that gravity is present wherever the mass of an object warps the fabric of space-time (Rothman & Sudarshan, 1998). Our planet is massive enough to bend space-time around it, so should we blame the Earth for the falling chicken? But how did Earth get here? Couldn't one argue that it was simply trapped by the even more massive gravitational effects of the sun? Clearly, the sun is to blame. Or as a better option, should we simply blame a parent or sibling for cramming the freezer too full?

Causal reasoning is fraught with pitfalls. We may choose an apparent cause instead of a true one, we may give more weight to a contributing factor than it deserves, or we may assume that mere correlation implies causation (recall the mountain lion). Our reasoning is likely to be particularly clouded when we look back in time from an event and attempt to locate a cause. This type of faulty reasoning is called *post hoc reasoning*, which is derived from the Latin phrase *post hoc, ergo propter hoc*, which taken literally means "after this, therefore because of this."

Scientific experiments try to correct the problems involved in isolating causes. The conditions of a scientific investigation manipulate variables so that genuine causes can be isolated from apparent but false causes. In many sciences, statistical tests are used to differentiate between major and minor causes while accounting for the probability that events may happen by chance alone. The "law" of cause and effect is a true conundrum: A chain of events may seem quite obvious in daily life, but it may prove maddeningly elusive if we try to develop meaningful explanations for the many complex phenomena that surround us.

We began this chapter by examining how valid forms of deductive arguments force us to accept the truth of their conclusions. Like a geometric proof, the form of a valid deductive argument will always transmit the truth of its premises to its conclusion. Inductive arguments are much less intrepid; they only aim to provide a conclusion that is *likely* to be true. Scientific theories are constructed out of inductive arguments, and are often extended (or rejected) by applying deductive arguments based on the premises of these theories.

We then looked at the special cases of correlation and causation. Serious errors may occur if we confuse mere correlation with causation, or if we reason backwards from an event to what we assume is its cause. We must be eternally vigilant in order to avoid such reasoning.

Other forms of reasoning, such as intuition and aesthetic analysis, do not claim to establish necessary conclusions. In their best manifestations, these methods are highly refined, scholarly opinions that seek to persuade, rather than to convince.

We must remember that the most important knowledge we generate is based on the two (often opposing) methods of deduction and induction, and on the all-too-fallible processes of correlating events and seeking causes. Thus, we would be wise to be humble when asked what we know for certain.

Classroom Activities and Assessments

The **Bigfoot Census Project Report** (pp. 48–57) provides students with practice in identifying invalid deductive arguments and inductive fallacies, presented in a fictitious report from a biased source. After working on this assignment, students should be able to separate arguments into premises and conclusions and evaluate premises to determine how well they support conclusions. Using **A Quick Guide to Common Fallacies and Invalid Deductive Arguments** (pp. 49–51), a resource guide, students should also be able to identify the following common fallacies:

- arguing from ignorance,
- using an unrepresentative sample,
- having a false dilemma,
- using circular reasoning,
- using post hoc reasoning, and
- confusing correlation with causation.

Finally, students will be required to identify two invalid deductive argument forms: affirming the consequent and denying the antecedent. These are also discussed in the provided resource guide. An **answer key** for the Bigfoot Census Project Report is provided on pages 59–60.

Letter to the Editor (p. 58; grading criteria on p. 61) is an assignment that asks students to adopt a biased point of view and write a letter to an editor. Students will be required to apply what they know about fallacious and invalid inductive and deductive arguments to make their claims both ridiculous and incredible. These letters are often fun to share aloud in class. After a student reads a letter aloud, ask which fallacies he or she used.

Bigfoot Census Project Report

Teacher Instructions

1. Give each student a copy of A Quick Guide to Common Fallacies and Invalid Deductive Arguments, found on pages 49–51.

2. Have students read the Field Report on pages 52–57. You may have individuals read to themselves or aloud, or have students read these pages in groups. Stress that what students are about to read is a fictitious field report designed to test their skills at identifying fallacies and bogus reasoning.

3. Students should underline examples of poor arguments and note these in the margins. They should then summarize the arguments on their own paper in a premise–conclusion format. An example of this, highlighting *post hoc* reasoning, is as follows:

> **Premise:** We didn't find any Bigfoot creatures.
> **Premise:** Bigfoot is afraid of dogs.
> **Premise:** One researcher brought a dog on a survey trip.
> **Conclusion:** The Bigfoot creatures stayed away because of the dog.

4. Discuss the results with students once they have finished. Please note that some arguments will not neatly fit into any single category, but breaking them down into premises and conclusions will help to determine whether they are valid.

5. Ask students whether the report relies on the accepted procedures of science. For example, how does it deal with data? Does it change its hypothesis based on the data, or does it change the data in order to fit a predetermined hypothesis?

6. You may wish to have students find an article or report in the media. Students should apply the same skills they used for this assignment: breaking the article or report down into premises and conclusions and then determining if it uses any identifiable fallacies or bogus logic.

A Quick Guide to Common Fallacies and Invalid Deductive Arguments

Inductive Fallacies

> A *fallacy* is a mistaken belief, especially one based on an unsound argument.

Appeal to Ignorance: Also called *argument from ignorance*, this fallacy states that something is true because nobody has ever proven it false (e.g., ghosts are real because nobody has proven that they aren't).

Circular Thinking: Somebody offers "proof" of an argument by stating the original claim in a slightly different way. In other words, the conclusion and premise(s) are essentially identical (e.g., ballet is difficult because it is hard to do; *difficult* and *hard to do* are synonyms).

False Dilemma: The reader or listener is forced to choose between only two options, when more than these two options exist. The author of the false dilemma will attempt to make his or her favored option the only attractive one of the two (e.g., either you are a vegetarian, or you believe in cruelty to animals).

Post Hoc Reasoning: This term comes from the Latin phrase *post hoc, ergo propter hoc*, or "after this, therefore because of this." This fallacy is committed when we reason backwards from an event and try to assume a cause. Many events may occur in chronological order without being at all causally related (e.g., worms come out after thunder, so thunder must scare them from their tunnels; rain, not thunder, causes worms to emerge).

Hasty Conclusion: This fallacy draws a conclusion based on insufficient or irrelevant information (e.g., deciding that Illinois is a dry state after spending only one week there, during which it did not rain).

Begging the Question: This fallacy is made when an author or speaker automatically assumes a conclusion is correct and then incorporates that conclusion into the premises of the argument (e.g., because she has avoided radar and sonar detection for decades, the Loch Ness Monster must be a very clever creature; because this author presumes the Loch

Ness Monster exists, he takes evidence that actually disproves the monster's existence and uses it to corroborate that it *does* exist).

Confusing Correlation and Causation: The arguer assumes that two things occurring at the same time or in the same place must be causally related (e.g., the price of small cars goes up, and the number of people flying goes down; neither of these necessarily caused the other, and both may have been influenced by a third factor, such as high fuel prices).

Invalid Deductive Arguments

> The conclusions of invalid deductive arguments are not necessarily true, even if the premises are. Two common forms of invalid deductive arguments are listed below.

Affirming the Consequent: The structure of this invalid form may be symbolized as follows:
- If P, then Q.
- Q.
- Therefore, P.

An example will illustrate why this form of deduction does not guarantee true conclusions. Consider this argument:
- If the beverage is coffee, then it has caffeine.
- The beverage has caffeine.
- Therefore, the beverage must be coffee.

Many other beverages have caffeine. The mystery beverage *may* be coffee, but it may also be another caffeinated drink, such as soda or hot chocolate. This type of invalid argument takes a given result and assumes a definite cause, although that cause is really only one of multiple possible causes.

Denying the Antecedent: This is another common deductive error. Its structure may be symbolized as follows:
- If P, then Q.
- Not P.
- Therefore, not Q.

An example illustrates the problems with this form.

- ⚙ If Jim is a Methodist, then he is a Christian.

- ⚙ Jim is not a Methodist.

- ⚙ Therefore, Jim is not a Christian.

Even though this conclusion may be true—for instance, Jim may be a Buddhist—and both premises may be true, the argument still does not make sense. This type of invalid argument assumes that because one condition in the premises is false, the conclusion will be as well. The mistake lies in overlooking the fact that categorically rejecting one condition (being a Methodist) does not toss out the conclusion. After all, the set of people who are Christians is larger than the set of people who are Methodists.

Name: _____ Date: _____

CLASSIFIED

Field Report
Bigfoot Census Project,
Northern Cascades, Washington

Background and Methodology

Researchers: Calvin Goldblum, M.A., and Renee Saunders-Janson, Psy.D., founders of The Bigfoot Preservation and Legal Advocacy Service, P.O. Box 734, Klishmatahoshik, WA. Assisted by interns Clark "Yeti Man" Porter, James "Howlin' Jim" Girsch, Jay Gould, and Fiona Ziegfried.

Location: Mount Baker-Snoqualmie National Forest

Purpose of Study: The purpose of the Bigfoot Census Project was to establish reasonable population-density estimates for the elusive North American primate commonly referred to as Bigfoot or Sasquatch. The project's ultimate goal is to establish the North American Bigfoot as an endangered species and to preserve a habitat for these majestic creatures.

Methods: The researchers, who have 25 years of combined experience in Bigfoot field research and education, embarked on this project on June 17, 2010. Using GPS technology and relief maps, the researchers crisscrossed an area composed of 36 square miles of the Mount Baker-Snoqualimie National Forest in the Cascade Range of Washington. Particular attention was paid to the Glacier Peak Wilderness Area, a remote portion of this pristine wilderness.

The survey was conducted over a period of 6 weeks, subdivided into 18 separate backcountry trips. Cross sections of the area were traversed in approximately 40-acre parcels, with each researcher responsible for either vertical or horizontal transects.

Researchers scanned the backcountry for any signs of Bigfoot presence, including but not limited to footprints, bedding areas, scat, disturbed underbrush, vocalizations, wood knocking (a common auditory signal of Bigfoot presence), and visual sightings. Regarding the aforementioned signals, the following assumptions were made:

⚙ Wood knocking or vocalizations indicated the presence of at least one Bigfoot, possibly a male protecting a family unit.

⚙ Footprints indicated the presence of one or more of the species.

- The estimated number of the species was proportionate to the extent of environmental disruption, bedding, bent underbrush, and/or scat.
- Visual sightings would yield a confirmed count.

Results of the survey indicated extant Bigfoot populations. These will be discussed in detail in the following section. For a more detailed account of methodology, please contact the Bigfoot Preservation and Legal Advocacy Service.

Results: The Pacific Northwest is noted for numerous Bigfoot sightings extending back into prehistory, as evidenced by Native American lore. Previous attempts have been made to spot, photograph, capture, or otherwise prove the existence of these elusive creatures. The present study was more modest in its goals, striving merely to use all possible evidence to determine a reasonable estimate of population density. The survey's results are summarized in the following section.

Summary of Data

Evidence	Survey trip no.	Sector no.*	Frequency, duration, or traits	Population estimate
Wood knocks (day)	3	6	20–50, duration 30 s	2
Wood knocks (night)	4, 6, 10, 17	7, 10, 30	20–70, duration 45 s	10
Vocalizations	12	5, 8	2 screeches, duration 5 s	3
Bedding sites	1	1	bent grass, leeward side, aspen grove	1
Footprints	18	34	2 prints in rocky clay (each showing 5 toes and a heel imprint)	1–2
Scat	2, 17	3, 32	dissolved by rains; contained berries and backpacker food; currently under laboratory investigation	2
Sightings	18	36	use of infrared camera on trail (possible leg; see report).	1
No evidence	5, 7, 8, 9, 11, 13, 14, 15, 16	2, 4, 9, 11–29, 31, 33		

*A detailed map of sectors may be obtained from the authors upon request.

Discussion and Commentary

Census Estimate: Results of the current field study indicate the presence of 19–21 Bigfoot creatures within the area surveyed. This may represent a higher density than that of other parts of the state and continent, as the northern Cascades are particularly remote and have historically served as the dominant Bigfoot habitat.

"No Evidence" Results: In 24 sectors, and on nine of the 16 survey trips, we found no sign of Bigfoot activity. (Let the unbiased nature of this report be proven by this admittance.) In retrospect, we believe that our presence may have been discovered and communicated among various communities of the animals, which may have increased their already-considerable wariness. This seems likely, given the fact that Sectors 11–29, where Bigfoot activity was not recorded, contains more meadows and open vistas than do the other sectors, enabling the creatures to see us at a distance and hide quickly.

It is worthy of note that one of the volunteer investigators brought a dog along with her on Trips 11, 15, and 16. It is well known that Bigfoot creatures are wary of dogs and will avoid areas where dogs may be heard barking. After both trips that yielded no Bigfoot evidence, several volunteers (on numerous occasions) commented that the dog appeared to be acting strangely at night.

Wood Knocking: Wood knocking sounds were heard in the forest on several trips and in many sectors. Although none was accompanied by a sighting, the fact remains that the source of the knocks could be neither identified nor observed, leaving the source of the noises unclear. Skeptics often attribute wood-knocking noises to woodpeckers or blowing branches; however, this phenomenon begs further investigation.

It is well known within the Bigfoot research community that Bigfoot will often strike trees or stumps with larger branches, presumably as a warning or to communicate the presence of humans to nearby creatures. (Other primates behave similarly.) Therefore, regarding the current data, our reasoning is as follows:

- If Bigfoot creatures are present, then we will hear wood knocks of no observed origin.

- We heard wood knocks of no observed origin on five occasions.

- Therefore, Bigfoot creatures were present on these occasions.

Vocalizations: The same researcher heard two vocalizations (in two sectors). These events occurred on Trip 12. Each vocalization consisted of a drawn-out, screeching noise that grew in volume towards the end. This was heard from quite a distance, and its location was difficult to determine due to echoes and wind. The researcher was unable to record the vocalizations, and the presence of owls and foxes in the area has not been established. Regardless, the researcher reported that he had never heard owls make such noises.

In spite of the relatively limited data set, we have concluded that the noises most likely originated from an adult male Bigfoot attempting to protect his territory. The presence of copious excrement in a nearby sector supports this conclusion.

Bedding Site: Given the reported Bigfoot activity in the area of the study, we had hoped to find more than one bedding site. The fact that we found only one proves how intelligent these creatures are. During sleep, a vulnerable time for animals, they know where they can avoid being detected.

Potential bedding sites that contained deer droppings were ruled out. The site we found did not contain any tracks or droppings from other animals. Because a site of this type, and in this location, is either a deer site or a Bigfoot site, and because we did not find signs of deer, we determined that this site must have been made by Bigfoot.

Footprints and Scat: Both footprints and scat, or excrement, are common signs of an animal's presence and are used in the field to determine populations. Two footprints were found in fairly rocky clay that had been softened by rain. The footprints were near one another, with one farther ahead, indicating a walking animal. Although the prints were similar to those a bear would make, we concluded that they were not bear prints due to the following:

- ⚙ If at least four prints had been found, the tracks would have been those of a walking bear.

- ⚙ We did not find four prints.

- ⚙ Therefore, the tracks were not those of a bear.

Because the prints were either bear tracks or Bigfoot tracks, we have no other option but to regard the tracks as those of a Bigfoot.

Scat is less easy to attribute to one species, as many creatures thrive on the same foods. A Bigfoot, being a large creature and likely related to other primates, would probably be an omnivore with a largely herbaceous diet. (Bears and raccoons have similar diets.) The scat we found contained large amounts of freeze-dried juice powder and biscuit mix. On both trips on which scat was found, we encountered backpackers who reported that something had crept into their campsites at night and rummaged through their food supplies. The backpackers had hung their supplies in suspended "bear bags" to protect the food. However, in both instances, the bags were torn down. Bigfoot creatures are tall enough that a theft of this nature would be possible for them to commit. Given the presence of other Bigfoot signs in this region, we were left to conclude that Bigfoot creatures scavenge from campsites when possible.

> **Given the presence of other Bigfoot signs in this region, we were left to conclude that Bigfoot creatures scavenge from campsites when possible.**

Bigfoot Sighting: We have reserved our most exciting finding for last. An infrared camera with slow-speed film and a motion-sensitive shutter was mounted on a tripod beside a trail for two nights. The trail was near a meadow and a natural spring. Unfortunately, on the second night, the wing nuts on the tripod legs spontaneously loosened (or were loosened by someone or something) and the camera slid downward. Much to our dismay, this was the night that gathered the most interesting evidence. Movement triggered the camera, causing it to snap a picture of what appears to be a hairy leg.

Because the leg, upon close examination, resembles a primate leg, we believe that it shows the leg of a Bigfoot. Unfortunately, the camera was damaged in transit from the high country camp where this study was conducted. As a result, digital images cannot be sent to a lab for further analysis. We plan to return to the same site in the future and set up five cameras at promising locations.

Avenues for Further Research: We hope to use evidence from this study on subsequent research journeys into the Cascades. We will return to Sectors 7, 10, 30, 5, 8, 3, and 32. A bear bag will be suspended from branches at two campsites in Sector 10. Infrared motion-sensing cameras will be trained on the bag to capture images of Bigfoot creatures, should they choose to steal food again.

We are especially interested in finding more bedding sites. We believe that a low-level aerial survey of prime locations will make the search more efficient. We also believe that remaining in one place for a week or more, along with engaging in wood knocking, will eventually attract curious Bigfoot creatures. We also wish to look for more substantial shelters than bedding sites. These creatures need to find sturdy, dry shelters in which to raise their young. The bedding site found in this study seemed to be temporary and reserved for a single creature, rather than a family.

The Ultimate Evidence: A growing number of skeptics criticize Bigfoot research efforts. Most point out that no one has found a Bigfoot corpse despite reports that the animal may stand in excess of 7 feet tall. Others point out that photographic evidence is unconvincing, labeling the famous Patterson/Gimlin video a hoax.

We recognize that a corpse, a part of a corpse, or a picture would provide the most conclusive possible evidence. We certainly do not possess the sort of evidence that would satisfy skeptics. However, we may respond to the naysayers by pointing out that no one has yet conclusively disproven the existence of Bigfoot. Therefore, we believe that we are fully justified in assuming that this magnificent, elusive creature lives in the wilds of North America. We remain confident that future research will prove our theory.

Letter to the Editor

Using extra paper as needed, write on the following prompt. You must use **both** faulty deductive reasoning and faulty inductive reasoning to support your conclusions. You should include an introduction, reasoning, and a conclusion in your article.

> **Role:** Biased writer
> **Audience:** General public
> **Format:** Letter to the editor of a local newspaper
> **Topic:** Any ridiculous claim you wish to make (e.g., "Cows talk when nobody is looking"; "Fluoridated water calms the American public, making citizens follow leaders peacefully")

Bigfoot Field Report
Answer Key

Discussion and Comments

"No Evidence" Results: Post hoc reasoning was used here to justify not finding Bigfoot creatures. The terrain and the presence of a dog were cited as causes after the fact. Students would also be correct to point out the fallacy of **confusing correlation with causation**. Yes, the dog was present, but no causal relationship existed.

Wood Knocking: The bulleted portion of the report regarding wood knocking is an example of **affirming the consequent**, an invalid deductive argument form. (The wood knocks could have come from many other unseen sources.) The second premise does not guarantee, or even confidently support, the conclusion.

Vocalizations: Here, the authors arrive at a **hasty conclusion**. They have insufficient data.

Bedding Site: This section of the report commits two fallacies. First, rather than accepting the data as they are presented, the authors assume that a lack of bedding sites proves that more Bigfoot creatures are hidden. Because they have begun with the conclusion that they intend to prove (in spite of evidence), they are guilty of **begging the question**. The second fallacy is a **false dilemma**. The authors state that the site must be either for deer or for Bigfoot, not considering any other possibilities.

Footprints and Scat: The bulleted portion of the report regarding footprints and scat is an example of the invalid logical form **denying the antecedent**. This section also contains a **false dilemma** and a **hasty conclusion** based on an insufficient or inaccurately obtained sample.

Bigfoot Sighting: The authors are guilty of **circular reasoning**, essentially saying that they believe the leg is a Bigfoot leg because it looks like one.

Avenues for Further Research: The authors continue to display their biases but use no fallacies or invalid forms of argument.

The Ultimate Evidence: The authors employ an **appeal to ignorance** by claiming that the creature exists simply because it has not been proven *not* to exist.

Entire Report: Make sure students also notice how the entire Bigfoot report **begs the question**. The authors never once question whether Bigfoot exists. Instead, they begin with this conclusion and then evaluate all of their data through this lens. Indeed, they want the data to fit their theory, instead of having their theory encompass the data. This is often a symptom of pseudoscience, a field of inquiry that pretends to be scientific. The authors refer to their theory; however, they do not really possess a theory. Instead, they have a preexisting bias that they want the data to support. Theories are generated to *explain* data, and when data refute theories, then theories—not data—are modified.

Letter to the Editor

Grading Criteria

The editorial article should meet the following criteria (5 points possible for each item):

✿ The article should follow a three-part format, with an introduction, a body, and a conclusion.

_____ points

✿ Each point or conclusion the student makes should have premises supporting it.

_____ points

✿ The article should include at least one inductive argument.

_____ points

✿ The student should use at least one deductive argument.

_____ points

Total points (out of 20): _____

Comments:

_____

_____

- -

Make Up Your Mind © Prufrock Press

Name: _____ Date: _____

Letter to the Editor

Grading Criteria

The editorial article should meet the following criteria (5 points possible for each item):

✿ The article should follow a three-part format, with an introduction, a body, and a conclusion.

_____ points

✿ Each point or conclusion the student makes should have premises supporting it.

_____ points

✿ The article should include at least one inductive argument.

_____ points

✿ The student should use at least one deductive argument.

_____ points

Total points (out of 20): _____

Comments:

_____

_____

- -

Make Up Your Mind © Prufrock Press

CHAPTER 5

Absolutism vs. Relativism

Objectives

- Students will compare two major conceptual foundations for determining what behavior is ethical and what behavior is unethical.

- Students will deconstruct ethical conflicts arising from cultural differences.

- Students will analyze the relative merits of relativist, deontological, and absolutist ethics.

- Students will evaluate current controversies stemming from the conflict between absolute and relativist ethics.

- Students will create an ethical dilemma.

Introduction

Imagine reading a newspaper account about a young man in Borneo who was recently arrested for murdering a man in a neighboring village. Furthermore, you read that the murderer removed his victim's head and took it back to his house, where it was found buried in the backyard when authorities arrested him. This, you think, was a gruesome criminal act.

Now imagine reading a later news report stating that the young man in Borneo belonged to a tribe that still, for some occasions, practices headhunting. This custom has been a part of the tribe's culture for thousands of years. The young man's tribe was in conflict with a neighboring village, and he was part of a small party of men retaliating against an earlier skirmish, wherein their village was attacked. A lawyer defending the man pointed out that at least 30 other men in his village had taken heads, and that the young man's great grandfather was regarded as one of the most powerful men in the tribe, having taken more than 15 heads in his lifetime. The lawyer went on to point out that tribesmen bury the heads in the graves of their ancestors so that the spirits of the dead can be servants to their deceased relatives in the afterlife. The young man who was arrested had buried the head in his grandfather's grave. Although the young man's behavior was definitely unlawful, as well as being decidedly gruesome, is it still as *criminal* as it first appeared?

This fictional situation has real-life parallels. Long ago, colonial authorities banned headhunting in Borneo and other areas of Indonesia. Most residents no longer practice their former religions, and headhunting has been replaced by less violent rituals. However, headhunting incidents have been reported during times of conflict and tension (Spillius, 2001).

Are certain actions *always* morally wrong, regardless of circumstances and time period? Or does the "rightness" or "wrongness" of a particular action depend upon the circumstances? Those who believe that some acts are always right or wrong, regardless of the circumstances, are *absolutists*. They believe in the absolute nature of particular actions. In contrast, those who believe that the ethical nature of particular actions is dependent on surrounding circumstances are often called *relativists*. They believe that acts cannot be declared right or wrong, ethical or unethical, until the setting in which they occur is taken into account. According to moral relativists, a person's actions can only be relatively right or relatively wrong; the ethics of the situation depend upon the actor, the setting, and other circumstances.

Ethical relativism has been the unofficial stance of those in the social sciences, particularly in cultural anthropology. In 1947, the American Anthropological Association lobbied the United Nations (UN) Commission on Human Rights, asking the organization to take a relativistic approach in its *Dedication of the Rights of Man* (Cook, 1999). They wanted the UN to issue a statement concerning the "rights of men to live

in terms of their own traditions" (p. 39). Luckily for those people who may live in cultures that do not recognize human rights, the Commission didn't listen.

Social scientists generally accept that morality is conditioned by culture. The community or group decides what is right or wrong. In the example, members of his own society would not regard the young man who beheaded the man in the neighboring village as having done anything ethically wrong. The killing of an enemy and the capture of the enemy's head as a valued trophy is—or at least, used to be—fully sanctioned by the culture. Although they may not condone the man's actions, ethical relativists would assert that the headhunter's actions, because they are sanctioned by his society, do not make him an unethical person.

Relativism in the social sciences has, according to many, crept into our general views on morality. We are reminded that different cultures have different values and practices (most of which are far milder than headhunting). Furthermore, we have been educated to accept these cultural values and practices. Indeed, relativism serves as a cornerstone for multiculturalism—our effort to understand others and produce both tolerance and acceptance of people who may be very different from us.

Although relativism may be essential in developing respect for diverse cultures, it also presents a major problem: It reduces morality to simply what the norm may be in some particular situation. Likewise, what may seem morally abhorrent could be regarded as simply being outside of the norms of a given culture. For example, a relativist would have to regard morally horrifying practices such as human sacrifice in ancient Central America, slavery in colonial Virginia, and Nazi concentration camps as expressions of particular cultures during particular times. According to relativism, we cannot objectively judge these practices. A purely relativist thinker would be forced to argue that it is our culture that has taught us to regard these events and practices as immoral; he or she would say that if we understood the people and the time periods associated with these events and practices, then we would not be so hasty to pass judgment.

It is ironic that relativism, the construct that allows us to embrace diverse cultures without falling prey to prejudice, renders us unable to pass judgment on those who practice prejudice. For instance, a radical relativist would not condemn the actions of a racially bigoted segregationist from a 19th-century Mississippi hamlet. The bigot simply acted as he was taught to act, the relativist would say. According to the relativist, this example shows not crime, but rather a provincial attitude and ignorance of other ways of thinking.

Indeed, the more one becomes grounded in relativism, the less one can condemn (or endorse) anything that people do—and people have done some horrible things. It may be cognitively useful, but relativism is inherently unsatisfying as a moral stance.

This brings us to absolutism. Absolutists disagree with the "wishy-washy" views of relativists; they argue for the existence of universal moral rules that are objectively true and knowable. Absolutists say that we can declare some actions immoral—and moreover, that we can base our judgments on universal principles. For example, an absolutist may point to the fairly universal nature of "The Golden Rule": Do unto others as you would have others do unto you. If somebody applied this maxim to slavery or headhunting, then that person would be forced to admit that those practices were unethical. In the headhunter example, for instance, an absolutist might claim that because the young man would not have wanted his own head cut off, his action was empirically wrong.

There are problems with absolutism as well, and there are various types of absolutists. For example, some claim that ethical rules come to us from God or exist as part of nature (i.e., natural law). Others claim that ethical rules can be deduced by rational beings (i.e., without invoking any deity). Still others claim that universal ethical principles may be found in our inborn desire to seek pleasure and avoid pain (White, 1997). Absolutists may disagree with one another as frequently as they disagree with relativists!

Critics have pointed out that as much as absolutists would like to possess a fully reasoned set of rules that could be applied to all thorny moral issues, such formulae are usually dry and dispassionate. Moral choices may be more subjective, more psychologically conditioned, and more society-based than any set of rules can reflect. For instance, a boy faced with the temptation to tip over a garbage can on Halloween night will probably not go through an organized set of remembered rules. Instead, his moral dilemma will be experienced as a chaotic swirl of thoughts, emotions, environmental stimuli, and competing motives.

Finally, critics have pointed out that absolutist ethics have been used to justify immoral behavior (Robinson & Garratt, 1996). For instance, millions of indigenous people throughout the world were displaced and enslaved under the banner of "the White man's burden." This term, coined in 1899 by poet Rudyard Kipling, referred to the supposed duty Europeans had to educate and uplift non-White people who had not been "blessed" with their religion and culture (particularly British religion and culture). The Nazis, of course, had their own set of absolutist principles. Their belief in certain universal principles permitted the

extermination of millions of Jews under a regime supported by ordinary citizens—ostensibly, not all of these citizens were absolutely evil.

So how should we decide whether actions are ethical or unethical? Relativism forbids us to state that any behavior, no matter how noble or horrible, is anything other than a cultural norm. Absolutism may give us the comfort of relying on universal ethical principles, but there are many types of absolutism, none entirely satisfactory, and absolutism has provided excuses for terrible events in history.

It is difficult—maybe even impossible—to be both a relativist and an absolutist. Yet in spite of this apparent contradiction, we find examples of both types of thinking everywhere, from the courts, to international politics, to the media. For example, in America, we will find people who are motivated by moral absolutes when condemning abortion, saying that innocent lives will be lost—yet many of these people may find nothing inconsistent in their support of an extensive nuclear arsenal, which presumably could result in the deaths of many innocent people. Likewise, we also find people who use relativist arguments when supporting the choice of abortion, yet are vehemently opposed to the death penalty. Neither group takes a consistent stance towards how we protect, approach, or even define our ethical commitments to human life.

Even our daily thoughts incorporate a chaotic mixture of relativism and absolutism, regardless of how much we may have studied this conundrum. The world of human choice refuses to yield to tidy explanations. To be stretched between the horns of this dilemma is to be truly human.

Classroom Activities and Assessments

Arranged Marriage (pp. 69–71; discussion and essay questions on pp. 71–73) is a discussion starter script that students can read aloud or act out in class. Students should use the script as a jumping-off point for discussions about cultural norms and ethical relativism. **The Lifeboat: A Dilemma for Discussion** (p. 76; teacher guide on pp. 74–75), which can be read in class by students, forces them to contrast and debate utilitarian and deontological (absolutist) ethics. Students will write responses to the reading in preparation for a classroom discussion. **Laws and Policies Investigation** (pp. 77–78; rubric on p. 80) requires students to research controversial situations or current events involving a clash between laws or policies; students must also consider the ethical choices of those who have to abide by those laws or policies. Finally, **Ethical Dilemma Tic-Tac-Toe** (p. 79; grading criteria on p. 81) requires students to select three tasks that have them explore ethical dilemmas. General **Relativism vs. Absolutism Essay Questions grading criteria** are provided on page 82.

Arranged Marriage

> **Characters:** Najia, Allie, and Sarah, all seniors at a Chicago high school (Najia is a recent immigrant from Afghanistan; Allie and Sarah have grown up in Chicago.)
> **Scene:** The school cafeteria

Allie: The lettuce looks pretty wilted today. I'm leaving it alone.

Sarah: Me, too. You should have seen the salad bar at Bard State. That cafeteria had everything—even a place where you could mix your own stuff and get it cooked in a giant wok.

Najia: Are you definitely going to Bard?

Sarah: I think so. They offered me the best scholarship so far.

Allie: Take it, girl! Are the boys cute?

Sarah: I noticed a few who met my high standards. How about you, Najia? What are you going to do next year?

Najia: Get married.

Allie and Sarah: *(shocked)* What?

Najia: My father doesn't want me to study anymore. He knows a man who is coming here. His name is Junaid—he is a friend of my uncle. He's from my grandmother's village and attended university in Pakistan.

Allie: Do you know him?

Najia: Enough, I think. He is an engineer, and his first wife died last year. He talked with me for a little while the last time he was in the country. He's very shy.

Sarah: First wife? How old is he?

Najia: A little under 30.

Sarah: But that's as old as Mr. Lathrop!

Allie: *Eww.* Mr. Lathrop? Don't bring him up in the same sentence as marriage!

Sarah: I'm not talking about Mr. Lathrop, silly! I'm just saying . . .

Najia: *(becoming annoyed)* What? That I should not marry a man who is almost 30?

Sarah: I'm sorry . . . it's just that I don't get it. I mean—

Najia: In my country, girls get married earlier. And I cannot question my father. He knows me, and he knows who will make a good husband for me.

Allie: But don't you want to go to school? You're the smartest one in our senior biology seminar.

Najia: When I came here, I wanted to be a nurse. But that was before—things change.

Allie: Does this Junaid person *want* to get married to you?

Najia: Yes, Junaid told my father he would like to marry me.

Allie: But didn't anyone ask you? And what about becoming a nurse first? Can't you wait or something?

Najia: No, nobody asked me outright—and as far as being a nurse, that will be up to Junaid later on. For now, my father has made his decision. He even paid for part of Junaid's ticket this time. He thinks Junaid is very smart and kind.

Sarah: What about your mom? What does she think?

Najia: She agrees with my father. Maybe they talked—I don't know.

Allie: If you told your mom that you didn't want to get married right away, would she talk to your dad about it?

Najia: She might, but it wouldn't do much good if he's already made up his mind. I know he likes Junaid, and he says Junaid will be rich soon—that he is a good engineer. We have known his family for a long, long time.

Allie: But what about you? I don't get it. I don't understand how this . . .

Najia: Well, my mother and father say they don't understand you and Sarah. They said they would never have let me go to that concert in Warrenton, like you did. They also worry about you.

Sarah: Worry about us?

Najia: Yes. They like both of you a lot. They worry that no good man will want to marry you. Father said the good men would worry about your reputations, and my mother wonders why your fathers and brothers do not look after you.

Allie: Whoa there! I don't need my dad looking after me, and my moron brother can't even handle looking after his pet snake!

Sarah: My *reputation*? I don't have a reputation!

Najia: Don't be mad. My parents really like you. But don't you see? Their ideas differ from yours.

(during a phone conversation between Sarah and Allie later that evening)

Sarah: Could you believe that stuff Najia said today?

Allie: That was crazy talk! We should tell a school counselor about it. Maybe a counselor could go over to Najia's house and, like, plead her case?

Sarah: Good idea. Najia's got to go to college—she's way too smart just to get married.

Allie: Yeah! And to an older guy she doesn't even know? Jeez, it's like she's getting forced into it and she's afraid to tell us.

Sarah: Maybe she *is* afraid. She never did say what she wanted to do. It was like she gave up, or she was hiding something. Her dad can't decide for her!

Questions:

1. Should Allie and Sarah intervene and tell a counselor?

2. If you were the counselor and Allie and Sarah came to you, what would you say or do?

3. Why didn't Najia complain? Is she being forced into marriage?

4. Does Najia want to marry Junaid?

5. What rules and expectations for school and marriage do Allie and Sarah have?

6. What rules and expectations for school and marriage does Najia's father have?

Arranged Marriage

Questions

Using extra paper as needed, answer the following questions with short essay responses. For each question, write one complete paragraph.

1. Has Najia been taught to follow a traditional role for women in her culture, or has she been brainwashed? Explain your answer.

_____

_____

_____

_____

_____

_____

_____

_____

_____

2. What is the difference between being taught and being brainwashed?

_____

_____

_____

_____

_____

_____

_____

_____

_____

_____

Answer only **one** of the following two questions with a complete paragraph:

1. If you believe that Najia has been brainwashed, you are probably an absolutist. What rule should be established or applied to make things fair for Najia and others like her?

_____

_____

_____

_____

_____

_____

_____

_____

2. If you believe that Najia has been taught to follow a traditional role, you are probably a relativist. Why is it important for Allie and Sarah to allow Najia's family to go ahead with their plans without interfering?

_____

_____

_____

_____

_____

_____

_____

_____

_____

The Lifeboat:
A Dilemma for Discussion
Teacher Guide

If you decide to conduct a discussion on an ethical dilemma, copy the scenario on page 76 and share it with students. This dilemma pits two major ethical theories against one another. The first of these theories is utilitarian and relativistic, while the other focuses on ethical commands and is absolutist.

How you solve the lifeboat dilemma depends a great deal on whether you choose to look at the consequences of your actions, or to concentrate on the "commandments" that require you to behave in a certain way. On one hand, sacrificing the stowaway and saving the scientist will preserve more lives in the future. On the other hand, many people follow the Bible (and secularly, the Golden Rule), which commands us not to commit murder. Of course, whether sacrificing one life to save two is the same as murder is up for debate.

In this scenario, *utilitarian* ethics are in opposition to *deontological* ethics. A utilitarian would state that given a choice, the action that produces the greatest good for the greatest number of people is the preferable option. In the case of the lifeboat, this would mean sacrificing the stowaway, which would be the best option for the most people.

The word deontological comes to us from the Greek word *deon*, which means "obligation" or "duty." Clearly, if you strongly believed in your duty not to commit murder, you would refrain from shooting the stowaway, no matter how many lives you would save by preserving the scientist. There are two main deontological systems of ethics. The first—and most common—is the use of religious principles. Some call this divine command theory (White, 1997). The majority of humans will turn to religious principles for justification or guidance during difficult ethical decisions. Immanuel Kant, a quirky German philosopher, developed the second deontological system of ethics. He proposed two rules that one should follow in all ethical situations. The first rule says that you should act only if you are willing to have the "rule upon which you act" become a universal law; and the second says you should "act in such a way that you always treat humanity, whether in your own person or in the person of any other, never simply as a means, but always at the same time an end" (Stumpf, 1983, pp. 307–308). Kant said that rational beings should follow these laws, which excluded animals.

We can see that it would not matter if the navigator of the lifeboat were a rabbi or an atheistic Kantian philosopher. (If the navigator were a rabbi, then divine command would prevent murder, whereas if the navigator were a Kantian philosopher, then sacrificing anybody on the boat would not only be an infeasible universal law, but would also treat the sacrificed person as a means to an end.) In both cases, a deontological navigator would probably not sacrifice anyone, and would instead simply allow all aboard the boat to die of thirst.

The lifeboat example is as dramatic and illustrative as it is unlikely. However, it uses a recipe that creates situations that will invariably cause friction between people with utilitarian values and people with deontological ones. The recipe goes as follows:

1. Place a helpless person or group in . . .

2. a situation in which there is a shortage of a valuable resource, such that . . .

3. a choice must be made between one person or group and another person or group . . .

4. based on differing merits of each person or group . . .

5. and based as well on the likelihood of that person or group having a positive impact on the future.

The limited valuable resource is the most critical ingredient of this recipe; if there were ample resources, a decision would be simple or unnecessary.

A later assignment in this chapter will give students an opportunity to write their own utilitarian vs. deontological dilemmas. Help students construct their dilemmas around valuable resources and competing individuals (or groups) with varying characteristics. Consider resources such as medicine, donated organs, money, recognitions or awards, and clean water.

The Lifeboat

The good ship *Telos* hits a mine in shark-infested waters. Before the Captain goes down with the ship, he puts you—the navigator—in charge of a lifeboat, and he gives you a gun. On the boat with you are two other people: a famous scientist who is on the verge of developing a cure for cancer, and a stowaway who was found hiding in the ship's engine room. Before this journey, the stowaway was unemployed and supported himself by begging on the streets near the ship's port. Neither of these two people has a spouse or children.

As the days go by, you begin to run out of water. Soon it becomes clear that there will only be enough water for two people to make it alive—maybe—to the shipping lanes. The doctor and the stowaway agree that you must be spared, because you know the route to the nearest shipping lanes. However, the other two also know that one of them must be shot and killed. You are the captain of the lifeboat. You have three options: Your first option is to flip a coin; your second option is to choose who is shot and tossed overboard; and your third option is to do nothing, allowing everybody aboard to perish.

It occurs to you that you will make a big impact on the world if you sacrifice the stowaway and save the scientist, whose discoveries could save hundreds of thousands of lives each year. However, you are not sure that you should make such a decision. Can you really play God with the two lives in your boat? Perhaps the stowaway will make a great contribution to the world in the future. Flipping the coin would allow fate (or God) to decide. Finally, you have other doubts. Aren't all lives of equal value? Isn't sacrificing the life of the stowaway—or the scientist, for that matter—simply murder? Should the stowaway die simply because his life didn't turn out as successfully as the scientist's life? Maybe all of you should perish. But if all three of you died of dehydration, the world would still be robbed of the scientist's discoveries, along with any contributions that either you or the stowaway eventually made to the world.

What should be done?

Write a one-paragraph response to clarify your thinking and prepare for a classroom discussion.

_____

_____

_____

_____

_____

_____

_____

_____

Laws and Policies Investigation

Laws are rules established by our society. We are required to follow these rules, and we may face serious consequences if we do not. Policies aren't as strong as laws, but they are rules that must be followed. Most employers have policies, as do school systems, universities, and other public institutions. As with laws, a person may end up being punished if he or she does something that violates a policy.

Laws and policies are meant to be as concrete as possible. We want to be able to rely upon them to guide our actions; therefore, we want them to be clear, applicable to all situations, and absolute. People also want laws and policies to be fair; therefore, we want those who enforce them to be sensitive to our unique situations. Because of this, we also want laws to be relativistic in how they may be applied. This contradiction—between our desire for absolute laws or policies and our equally strong desire for fairness and understanding—leads to many controversies. Generally, these debates involve arguments about whether or not a law or policy can be applied to a particular situation (or all situations) and remain fair.

In sum, controversies often arise when absolute laws and policies meet relativistic situations. Most people want laws and policies to be firm, to protect us from wrongdoers. However, people also want laws and policies to be fairly applied to their unique situations; they often point out how the rules don't apply to their special circumstances and say that punishment is not deserved.

Using the form provided, complete an investigation:

1. Investigate a controversy between an absolute law, rule, or policy and a relativistic situation.

2. List the major arguments on both sides of the controversy.

3. State your position on the issue and support it, writing a minimum of three paragraphs.

> **Possible Controversial Topics/Issues**
> You might choose to investigate mandatory drug sentencing, zero-tolerance policies for weapons in schools, euthanasia, the death penalty, immigration laws, affirmative action, Title IX in sports, free speech protection, the torture of terrorists, the Geneva Convention and guerilla warfare, greenhouse gas rules for developing countries, stem cell research, or cloning.

Describe the issue and the law or policy that applies:

_____

_____

_____

Why and how does this issue (and its laws and policies) involve absolutism vs. relativism?

_____

_____

_____

What arguments can you make in favor of the law or policy?

_____

_____

_____

What arguments can you make in opposition of the law or policy?

_____

_____

_____

What is your position on the law or policy as it applies to the issue? Write at least three paragraphs. Use additional paper as needed.

_____

_____

_____

_____

_____

_____

_____

_____

_____

_____

_____

_____

_____

_____

_____

_____

Ethical Dilemma Tic-Tac-Toe

Read the tasks described in the boxes below. Complete any three that connect to make a horizontal, diagonal, or vertical line.

Write an ethical dilemma or dialogue featuring conflict between absolutism and relativism, or between utilitarian and deontological ethics.	Throughout the 18th and 19th centuries, American women were not allowed to vote. How would a relativist explain that this was an acceptable practice back then, but not today? Do you agree with this relativist explanation?	Racism has been a part of many cultures for thousands of years, yet virtually everyone agrees that racism is wrong. How would a relativist explain racism? What would an absolutist say? Who is more convincing, and why?
Write a brief (one-page) position paper describing whether you are a deontologist, a relativist, a utilitarian, or an absolutist. Explain why you chose the label you did.	Find an example of cultural relativism in the newspaper or printed in an online source. Write a paragraph explaining how it demonstrates relativism.	Write an ethical dilemma or dialogue featuring conflict between absolutism and relativism, or between utilitarian and deontological ethics.
Is belonging to a street gang wrong? (Assume that this gang commits crimes.) What would a relativist say? What would an absolutist say? With whom do you agree, and why?	Write a position paper on an ethical issue. In the paper, make sure to explain whether you are an absolutist, a relativist, a deontologist, or a utilitarian when it comes to this issue.	Make a chart comparing and contrasting **either** cultural relativism and absolutism **or** utilitarianism and divine command.

Laws and Policies Investigation

Rubric

	Poor	Adequate	Excellent
Choice of controversy to investigate	Doesn't apply to material or concepts being studied	Applies to concepts being studied	Provides a superior or original example of concepts
Explanation of role of absolutism vs. relativism	Does not offer evidence of comprehension	Offers evidence of comprehension	Engages in analysis of roles
List of major arguments	List is incomplete, perfunctory, or vague	List is complete and understandable	List is complete, thorough, and exceptional
Position on topic	Offers vague or obligatory position	States opinion and reasons	Position is persuasive and supported
Usage and mechanics	5 or more errors	2–4 errors	0–1 errors

Comments:

_____

_____

Ethical Dilemma Tic-Tac-Toe

Grading Criteria

	Poor	Adequate	Good	Excellent
Analysis and evaluation of concepts				
Organization				
Neatness, appearance				
Usage and mechanics				

Comments:

_____

_____

Name:_____ Date:_____

Ethical Dilemma Tic-Tac-Toe

Grading Criteria

	Poor	Adequate	Good	Excellent
Analysis and evaluation of concepts				
Organization				
Neatness, appearance				
Usage and mechanics				

Comments:

_____

_____

Name: _____ Date: _____

Relativism vs. Absolutism Essay Questions
Grading Criteria

	Poor	Adequate	Good	Superior
Analysis and evaluation of ideas				
Organization				
Neatness, appearance				
Usage and mechanics				
Other				

Comments:

_____

_____

Name: _____ Date: _____

Relativism vs. Absolutism Essay Questions
Grading Criteria

	Poor	Adequate	Good	Superior
Analysis and evaluation of ideas				
Organization				
Neatness, appearance				
Usage and mechanics				
Other				

Comments:

_____

_____

Discovered Math vs. Invented Math

Objectives

- ⚙ Using the Fibonacci series as a model, students will explore the curious connection between mathematics and the nature of reality.

- ⚙ Students will speculate about the source and nature of mathematical knowledge and its capacity to explain the world around us.

- ⚙ Students will apply spatial and mathematical solutions to create a Fibonacci-based design.

Introduction

Unfortunately, many people consider math merely an exercise in calculation. It is certainly important to know how to perform basic calculations. However, perhaps as the result of texts, tests, tradition, and teachers, people do not often contemplate how mysterious mathematics can be. It is as important to think *about* mathematics as it is to think *within* mathematics. Why is it that humans are able to think mathematically? Why does math seem to explain so much of our world? Was math invented, or is it a feature of the universe and its patterns that we have discovered? Out of all of the academic subjects, only mathematics was once a religion!

The first high priest of this mathematics-based religion was Pythagoras, born in the sixth century B.C.E. Pythagoras was an extraordinary mathematician and mystic who developed a devout following. He and his devotees came to believe that numbers were "living entities and universal principles, permeating everything from the heavens to human ethics" (Livio, 2009, p. 16). The Pythagoreans knew that numbers were useful—they counted on their fingers, like everyone else. However, they also believed that numbers were the foundation of the universe—that everything was ultimately composed of numbers. For them, numbers became a religion.

The Pythagoreans studied music, geometrical figures, and astronomy, identifying harmony, balance, and orderliness in the world (Valens, 1964). Today, we remember them mostly for Pythagoras's theorem concerning right triangles, a concept every geometry student learns. What isn't taught is the equally remarkable notion proposed by the Pythagoreans: the notion that humans do not create mathematics, but rather that they discover mathematics. For Pythagoras and his followers, mathematical principles were just as "real" as the physical world that we explore with our five senses, and thus they were (and continue to be) found, not invented.

An analogy would help to illustrate the genuinely remarkable mystery of numbers perceived by the Pythagoreans, a mystery that is still with us today. Imagine an explorer and cartographer, such as Captain James Cook. Nobody would say that the Hawaiian Islands did not exist prior to Cook's discoveries. The islands were always there; Cook did not draw them into existence with his ink and charts. Instead, we would say that with each discovery, Cook was able to develop his representation of what the mysterious islands looked like and how to navigate to them—things the Polynesians knew long before Cook!

The world of numbers may well exist just like Cook's tropical paradise did, simply awaiting our discovery. If this is true, then mathematics is not a creation of the human mind. Rather, it predates the human mind. We often hear the phrase "do the math." If mathematics exists independently of us, then it is more correct to say, "find the math."

Plato believed that mathematics was an extension of a heavenly, perfect realm—something he called the world of the forms. Plato regarded the world of the forms as an ideal, nonphysical, nontemporal reality. We can perceive and comprehend the world around us, and have ideas about it, because the forms mysteriously coexist with our temporal, physical,

and imperfect surroundings. For Plato, the only reason we can perceive or know anything is that all things we encounter (including concepts such as justice) have unique, perfect equivalents existing in the timeless world of forms.

Naturally, mathematics carried a special meaning for Plato. Here was a topic that had real-world examples, yet by reasoning from these examples, one could infer a flawless universal rule that could be applied to all situations. For example, we can measure the angles of a given triangle and find that they add up to 180 degrees. After measuring a few more triangles, we can arrive at a law that applies to all triangles. Indeed, it is as if there is an ideal triangle out there somewhere, and all triangles we encounter are a shadow of that triangle. We can find a rule that applies to all triangles because they are all reflections of the same "heavenly triangle." This is exactly what Plato thought!

Why can humans understand this about triangles, even those with little formal education about geometry? Plato maintained that prior to conception, our souls dwelled in the world of the forms, and that through intellectual effort, we could vaguely understand their perfection (Russell, 1954).

Plato's ideas, while fanciful, should not be regarded as ridiculous. Many mathematicians and philosophers have wondered why the human mind can understand mathematics, and why mathematics seems to be such a remarkable model of the world around us. Kurt Gödel, a brilliant mathematician and respected colleague of Albert Einstein, agreed with Plato. Einstein helped Gödel escape Nazi-occupied Austria and immigrate to the United States so that they could work together (Livio, 2009). Obviously, Einstein did not believe that Gödel was a lunatic.

The spiritual understanding of mathematics, as Plato and Pythagoras understood it, has not been universally accepted. The famous French mathematician Henri Poincaré maintained that abstract mathematical concepts, such as infinity, are without real meaning and may be influenced by the social and intellectual climate surrounding mathematicians. In other words, we create math and do not discover it (Shapiro, 2000). Numerous mathematicians have joined Poincaré in proposing that although mathematics is an elaborate system of thought, it is entirely made up by humans who extend propositions or bend formulas to suit their specific needs (Livio, 2009).

Anthropologists have studied the phenomenon of mathematics by introducing geometry and mathematics to hunter-gatherer societies that have not developed formal schooling. Although these people have some concept of numbering (which appears innate to human beings), they do not use complex systems such as Euclidian geometry. Researchers found that these systems were readily understood by people from primitive societies, but that they had not been spontaneously invented, leading to the conclusion that math may be an innate capacity that can be encouraged and extended by society, just like language or music.

Other criticisms exist of the supposed truth of mathematics. Some propose that mathematics is much like a runaway computer: Its accomplishments may be vast, but it remains blind to itself and its own creations. We may use language to explain how language came to be. However, mathematics is not capable of explaining itself (Livio, 2009; Shapiro, 2000). No mathematical system encompasses all branches of mathematics, and there is no successful mathematical theory of math. In some ways, mathematics is similar to chess. Once we have the board and pieces, the rules make sense. However, the rules cannot explain the existence of the board and pieces, nor can the rules predict all of the possible permutations of any game.

Given these limitations of mathematics, and its inability to explain itself as language can, it may be tempting to regard it as a faulty human invention. However, the essential mystery of mathematics remains intact, largely because of its role in science. How is it that something so abstract and intangible explains and predicts so much in the physical world? In other words, if mathematics were entirely a collection of mind games, it would not be such a useful tool for describing and modeling scientific theories.

It is one thing to label mathematics as invented when scientists make a discovery and then search for the math to describe their findings. It is quite another to do so when mathematicians come up with concepts and formulas that prove to be useful models for scientific discoveries years later, by other researchers from different cultures and continents! On numerous occasions, mathematicians have developed a particular mathematical concept simply as an exercise in pure math. Then, as if they had emerged from a crystal ball, the formulas and principles from this math turn out to provide the perfect model for science.

Two examples can help illustrate the mysteriously predictive power of mathematics. In the mid-19th century, a German geometry professor named Bernhard Riemann began experimenting with non-Euclidian geometry. In simplified terms, he examined the unique rules and principles that emerged from developing geometric figures on curved (not flat) planes. Almost 60 years later, this system of mathematics helped Einstein create a model for his general relativity theory, a theory that has

incredible explanatory power for everything from the warping of light in the universe to the operation of GPS satellites (Livio, 2009).

Beginning in the 19th century, other mathematicians started to explore ways to describe and classify the surfaces and relationships of knots (yes, knots!). It was this branch of mathematics that ended up, more than 50 years later, being the proper model for how enzymes disentangle strands of DNA so that RNA can do its work (Livio, 2009).

The 2,000-year-old debate over whether mathematics is discovered or invented will undoubtedly continue. Psychologists, anthropologists, and neuroscientists have entered into the discussion as well. Each new discovery, either in science or in math, challenges us to consider the remarkable powers of mathematics and the seemingly miraculous features of the human mind. Although we do not often consider it, our ability to understand the universe through mathematics remains an enduring enigma that is worthy of study.

Classroom Activities and Assessments

The Fibonacci numbers and the Golden Section are reviewed with **three lessons** (pp. 89–98) addressing the famed Fibonacci series. These lessons are designed to lead students towards an awareness of the mysterious ability of mathematics to describe and determine our world. The lessons require students to construct a Fibonacci (equiangular) spiral, comprehend the Golden Section and phi, and take a **comprehension quiz** (p. 99; answer key on pp. 102–103) covering related concepts. These lessons have been formatted as teacher instructions (Lesson 1 is simply background information, which may be copied, read aloud, or reviewed), but you can use them in whatever way is most helpful for your class. **Fibonacci Yard Art** (p. 101; grading criteria on p. 104) is an activity requiring students to problem solve in small groups. Students must use their knowledge of the equiangular spiral and the Fibonacci series to put together a proposal for creating a large-scale model.

Lesson 1: A Brief Introduction to Leonardo of Pisa

The Fibonacci series is named after one of the most famous mathematicians in Western history, Leonardo of Pisa, a 13th-century Italian who was nicknamed Fibonacci (a derivative of his father's nickname) by admiring townsmen. Fibonacci is largely credited with introducing the Arabic numeral system to medieval Europe, providing a huge advantage over the previous Roman numerals. He learned this system when he was a boy traveling with his father on business trips, trading with Moorish merchants throughout the Mediterranean. Later, he studied under the best Arabic mathematicians before returning to Italy, where he was invited to be in the Court of Frederick II.

Fibonacci first discovered the recursive series named after him when he was working on a problem involving how many generations it would take to produce a certain number of rabbits. In the centuries that followed, mathematicians developed the series and generalizations from it (Horadum, 1975). Like many discoveries in mathematics, what had first seemed like an interesting avenue to explore became an intellectual goldmine for later generations.

Lesson 2: The Fibonacci Series and Spirals

Materials

For this part of the lesson, you will need to provide a sheet of graph paper for each student, along with pencils (not pens). You will also need some way of drawing for the whole class—a whiteboard, an LCD projector, or an interactive screen.

Objectives

This portion of the lesson is designed to impress students with the unique ability of mathematics to model and describe features of the world. Students will learn specific facts about the Fibonacci series. At the end of this lesson, students will be able to do the following:

- create the Fibonacci series and describe one unique feature of it;

- briefly explain the history of the Fibonacci series;

- identify an equiangular spiral and define its features;

- explain the connection between an equiangular spiral and the Fibonacci series;

- describe at least three examples of an equiangular spiral occurring in nature; and

- evaluate unique parallels between the Fibonacci series and nature, especially in pinecones.

Procedure

The Fibonacci series is a simple number sequence that demonstrates remarkable properties. Entire books have been written on the series, and there are numerous Internet resources devoted to it.

> The Fibonacci series progresses like this: 0, 1, 1, 2, 3, 5, 8, 13, 21, 34 . . .
> Each number in this series (called a *recursive series*) is the sum of the two preceding numbers. The next number in the series after 34 would be 55, the sum of 34 and 21.

What is remarkable about the Fibonacci series is its mysterious connections to phenomena ranging from ideal proportions in landscape paintings to the population dynamics of honeybees. This lesson will not explore *all* manifestations of the Fibonacci series. You can find entire

books on this topic. Instead, the lesson will concentrate on basic features of the series, its connection to equiangular spirals, and where such spirals are found in nature.

The Fibonacci series has some unique properties. Before explaining these, present the table below to students:

n	0	1	2	3	4	5	6	7	8	9	10	11
Fib n	0	1	1	3	3	5	8	13	21	34	55	89

The top row (n) represents the ordinal position of numbers in the Fibonacci series, starting with zero. Essentially, the top row aligns a number line with the Fibonacci series. This row is designated by placing an "n" after the position number. Thus, 4n would represent the Fibonacci number 3.

If you add the squares of two successive Fibonacci numbers, the resulting number is also a Fibonacci. For example, $3^2 + 5^2 = 34$. Note that 3 is the fourth Fibonacci number (4n), and 5 is the fifth Fibonacci number (5n). Interestingly, summing these yields 9n (4n + 5n = 9n), or the ninth Fibonacci number . . . which is 34! Rather than squaring and summing the Fibonacci numbers to solve this equation, we can simply add the ordinal position (number line) numbers and find the corresponding Fibonacci number.

Another interesting feature of the sequence is that when you add all of the Fibonacci numbers up to a certain point and add one, that number will be the next in the series. For example, if you chose the Fibonacci number 3, the sum of all of the numbers in the series prior to 3 would be 0 + 1 + 1 + 2 = 4. Adding 1 to 4 equals 5, which is the next Fibonacci number after 3.

The Fibonacci Spiral

After you have played with the Fibonacci series, distribute one sheet of graph paper to each student. Their task involves making proportionally larger squares using the Fibonacci series (1 × 1, 1 × 1, 2 × 2, 3 × 3, 5 × 5, 8 × 8, and so on, following the series). The squares are then used as a guide for creating a spiral that is seen in many natural phenomena, ranging from galaxies to seashells.

Instruct students to take out pencils and move though the following steps:

1. Choose and outline one square unit (a single square on the graph paper) a little left of, and a little higher than, the center of the paper.

2. Select the square unit to the right of the one drawn in Step 1 and outline it.

3. Using the top side of the two square units now outlined, create a 2 × 2 unit square above the figures you have created.

4. Using the figures outlined, you are now ready to make a 3 × 3 square to the left of items you have outlined.

5. Continue this process in a counterclockwise fashion, making a 5 × 5 square below the one you just created (see illustration below). Use as much space as you have to keep making squares. Circulate and check with students to make sure they are doing the task correctly.

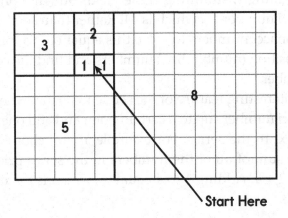

Once students have filled their papers as space allows, make sure they understand the connection between the progressive dimensions of the squares they have drawn and the Fibonacci series. After checking for comprehension, instruct students to connect the corners of the squares with arc sections (pictured below). They should continue until all outlined squares are filled.

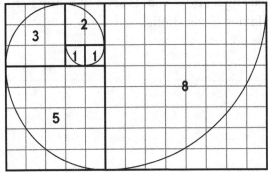

Discussion

The spiral students have designed is called an *equiangular spiral*. If it is drawn perfectly, it has some unique mathematical properties. Most notably, the angle end of each arc and the proportion of area covered in each square remain the same; only the dimensions increase as the spiral moves outward.

This arc can be seen throughout nature. (You can find many illustrations with an Internet search.) Some well-known examples are nautilus shells, snail shells, spiral galaxies, aloe plants, hurricanes, ram's horns, and the outward spirals of seed rows in sunflower heads (as well as in other flowers). The petals of many types of roses also follow this spiral.

Pinecones provide a fascinating connection between the equiangular spiral, Fibonacci numbers, and nature (Edkins, 2007). The seeds on a pinecone are called *bracts*. The following features are true for a majority of pinecones:

- The seeds grow in ascending (or descending) rows that spiral outwards from the tip.

- Plotting the spiral in two dimensions will yield an approximate equiangular spiral.

- Rows of bracts will "climb" from the base to the tip at a steeper angle; others will climb from the base to the tip in the opposite direction, at a more gradual angle. The total number of bracts in the steeper rows, as well as the total number in the gradual rows, will usually be adjacent Fibonacci numbers. For example, if the bracts in the steep rows total 34, then the total in the gradual rows will be 55 (two adjacent numbers in the Fibonacci series).

Other plants also follow the Fibonacci spiral. For instance, pineapple scales and palm tree bark rotate about their axes in spirals similar to those of pinecones. (There is a connection between plant structures and the Fibonacci series that is too involved for the purposes of this lesson.)

To demonstrate and illustrate these concepts for your students, find images of the following and distribute them or show them on a projector: nautilus shells, pinecones, pineapples, hurricanes, whirlpools, sprouting palm fronds, brocciflower (a cross between broccoli and cauliflower), ram's horns, spiral galaxies, tornadoes, and anything else you may find.

Additional Ideas and Notes

- ✿ When introducing the Fibonacci series, write the series on the board and have students determine which number will be next. Leave the series up as you explain some of the mathematical properties of the series.

- ✿ When using the graph paper, make sure that students start in the right place and are drawing correctly. They often make mistakes at the beginning of this demonstration. Make an example for students as you provide instructions.

- ✿ Spend time connecting the dimensions of the successive squares on graph paper with the Fibonacci series. Many students need help recognizing that the dimensions of the squares replicate the Fibonacci series.

- ✿ If you have access to an LCD projector or similar technology, you may access a variety of websites that illustrate the equiangular spiral, or Fibonacci spiral, of pinecones. Another powerful example takes some preparation time, but is well worth it. Find some pinecones and use tempura paint to color a gradual row of bracts yellow. Paint the opposing steeper row with another color. Pass these models around when teaching the concept.

- ✿ For homework, have students look for examples of the Fibonacci spiral either online or in nature.

Lesson 3: The Fibonacci Series and the Golden Section

Materials

For this lesson, you'll need an LCD projector, an interactive white board, posters, or some other form of visual display. Prepare a slideshow or use another method to present pictures to your class of an American flag, the *Mona Lisa*, a landscape painting or photograph using the rule of thirds, a Greek vase, pinecones, architecture photos (e.g., the Parthenon), and diagrams of dividing canvases and architectural plans into Golden Rectangles.

Objectives

The purpose of this second lesson is to draw a connection between the Fibonacci series and a very special irrational number designated by the Greek letter *phi* (pronounced *fie*, rhyming with pie). The Greek symbol for phi is ϕ, which represents approximately 1.61. By the end of this lesson, students will be able to do the following:

- ✿ demonstrate that phi is produced by the ratio of two adjacent Fibonacci numbers;

- ✿ identify examples of phi in architecture, design, painting, and photography;

- ✿ explain how pinecones generate phi;

- ✿ define and diagram a Golden Section and create a Golden Rectangle from a Golden Section;

- ✿ define an irrational number and apply this definition to phi; and

- ✿ hypothesize about the role of mathematics in aesthetics and nature.

Information and Instructions

Dividing adjacent Fibonacci numbers (dividing the larger by the smaller) will yield an irrational number called phi (ϕ). The number is *irrational* because it cannot be reduced to a fixed ratio. Instead, it continues as a nonrepeating decimal—just like another famous irrational number, pi. Generally, phi (1.61 . . .) is more closely approximated when larger Fibonacci numbers are used. For example, dividing 5 by 3 equals 1.667. However, dividing 55 by 34 equals approximately 1.618. Because the number is a nonrepeating decimal, we cannot really know what its true value is.

Phi is special because it also represents the value generated by dividing the larger of a line's two sections by the smaller of those sections when a line is divided into a proportion called the *Golden Section*.

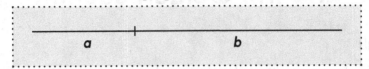

This line is a Golden Section because dividing the length of section *b* by the length of section *a* will equal around 1.61 (ϕ). Conversely, the ratio of *a* : *b* = 0.61. For those of you who may have forgotten what you knew about ratios, this simply means that section *b* is .61 times larger than section *a*, so multiplying *a* times 1.61, or ϕ, will equal *b*.

There is one other characteristic of a Golden Section. Just as the ratio of *a* to *b* equals .61, the ratio of *b* to (*a* + *b*) also equals .61. To put this in plain English, the ratio of the shorter section to the longer is the same as the ratio of the longer section to the total length of both sections.

The relationship of a Golden Section to phi is clear. The length of (*a* + *b*) divided by the length of *b* is equal to ϕ (or 1.61), and *b* divided by *a* is also equal to ϕ. It is as if phi is the DNA of the Golden Section!

The Golden Section is frequently used in art and photography. Instructors of landscape painting and photography warn students not to place an eye-catching object in the center of a picture. Instead, it is best to have the object approximately one-third from either the left or right edge. This divides the canvas into a Golden Section, with the object of interest separating the total width of the picture into sections whose ratio is equal to phi. There are hundreds of examples of how to divide a canvas or photograph. Many may be found online.

The Golden Section can also be converted into a rectangle, with the shorter section making two sides, and the longer making the other two.

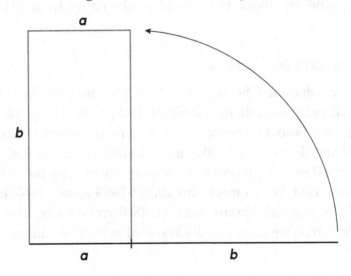

The resulting rectangle is called the Golden Rectangle. This, too, has been a common feature of art and architecture since the time of the Greeks. It is generally agreed that the Golden Rectangle has proportions that are most pleasing to the human eye. In DaVinci's *Mona Lisa*, the Renaissance beauty's face is framed perfectly by a Golden Rectangle. Many works of art and architecture use the Golden Rectangle as guide for proportions and spacing, including the Parthenon. Artists also divide canvases into areas of Golden Rectangles, and even the American flag is organized into Golden Sections. As a matter of fact, plotting the Fibonacci spiral can make a perfectly proportioned model of the embedded rectangles in the flag! (Students can examine this by looking at the graph-paper drawings they have already done, or by graphing a new set.)

Phi is observable in the proportions of vases and other objects. Often, these are perfectly framed by a Golden Rectangle, or they are divided proportionally into sections that approximate the Golden Section. You might instruct students to look for examples online, in stores, or in their own homes.

After students have had the opportunity to view several examples of the Golden Section and Golden Rectangle applied in art and architecture, draw their attention back to the pinecones from the previous lesson. Review the material to ensure they understand the ratio of the longer rows of bracts to the shorter row of bracts. (Again, these are likely to be adjacent Fibonacci numbers.) Connect this concept with today's lesson by helping students realize that the longer row of bracts divided by the shorter row will usually equal phi.

How intriguing it is to learn that hurricanes, galaxies, nautilus shells, pinecones, the *Mona Lisa*, the Parthenon, and the American flag are all united around the Fibonacci series and its offspring, phi! Many more connections can be made between phi and music, nature, plants, honeybees, and even the proportions of the human body. Take time to explore these with your class if you wish, helping students to recognize the mysterious nature of phi and why it appears in so many places.

Additional Ideas and Notes

- Define the term *irrational number* for students. An irrational number is defined as a real number that cannot be expressed as the quotient, or ratio, of two integers. It does not make a neatly divided or simple ratio, so it will continue repeating decimals infinitely and without a discernable order. The square root of 2 is an irrational number, as is φ.

⚙ Before beginning, make sure you are ready to display to your class the Fibonacci series, a diagram of the Golden Section, and a diagram of the Golden Rectangle. Make sure to label the long and short sections of the Golden Section and Golden Rectangle.

⚙ It is best to prepare images in advance, rather than running Internet searches in class prior to screening the results. Searching for "Golden Section" or "Golden Rectangle" produces a lot of artwork, some of which features nude figures.

⚙ You can use the numbers in the series for making models of the Golden Section for the class. Point this out to students and have them divide larger numbers in the series by smaller numbers to obtain phi. You can have them create examples using the series for dimensions.

⚙ Building off of students' drawings from the previous lesson, draw another set of squares following the Fibonacci series. This is a good way to review the concepts from the day before. Do not allow students to draw a spiral on the second sheet. Instead, show them how Golden Rectangles and Golden Sections are created when the graphed squares are joined. They will be able to see the exact spatial arrangement of the American flag.

Questions

1. Why do you think pinecones, the Parthenon, spiral galaxies, seashells, and many other things are connected with the Fibonacci series? What is the Fibonacci series capturing or describing?

2. Do you think differently about mathematics after learning about the Fibonacci series and Golden Rectangles?

3. Was the Fibonacci series invented or discovered? What is the difference? Defend and explain your answer.

The Fibonacci Series and the Golden Section: Comprehension Quiz

1. What is one unique feature of the Fibonacci series?

   _____

   _____

   _____

2. Using a diagram and written captions, explain how the Fibonacci series can be represented on a grid and transformed into an equiangular spiral.

3. List three examples of equiangular spirals in the natural world.

   _____

   _____

   _____

4. Explain how pinecones are "designed" around the Fibonacci series.

   _____

   _____

   _____

5. Fill in the missing Fibonacci numbers in the following sequence:

   8, _____, 21, _____, 55, _____, 144

6. Use two numbers in the series above to create phi. Show your work.

7. Assume that line segment AC, shown below, is a Golden Section. Circle any of the statements that are true.

A   B   C

BC ÷ AB = ϕ.

AB ÷ BC = ϕ.

AC ÷ BC = 1.61 . . .

The ratio of AB to BC is equal to the ratio of BC to AC.

If BC is divided in half, it can be used to make a Golden Rectangle.

If BC is divided by 1.61, it will equal (approximately) AB.

The dimensions of AB and BC can be used to make a Golden Rectangle.

8. Why is phi an irrational number? _____

   a) Because ϕ has the same value as π.
   b) Because it must be written as a decimal that repeats the same set of numbers.
   c) Because it cannot be completely expressed as a ratio.
   d) Because it is not related to the Golden Section.

9. Given what you now know about the Fibonacci series, the Golden Section, phi, and the Golden Rectangle, complete the sentence below. You may write a paragraph if you wish.

Math is like . . .

_____

_____

_____

_____

_____

_____

_____

_____

_____

_____

Fibonacci Yard Art

This architectural challenge requires you think deeply about the proportions and measurements of the equiangular spiral and solve a complicated problem. You need to work cooperatively with a partner and write a proposal for your project.

The Challenge

Using a can of spray paint, how could you make a giant equiangular spiral, or a design using equiangular spirals, in the yard outside of your school? An alternative assignment is to make a design on the school playground using sidewalk chalk.

Develop a plan for accomplishing this task. Your plan should include the following:

1. Step-by-step instructions

2. A diagram illustrating the process you propose

3. A sketch of the final product (sketches should include measurements showing how large the design will be—for instance, 16' x 16')

4. A list of the materials you will need

How You Will Be Graded

The most effective and workable plan will win the challenge. Make sure your instructions and descriptions are clearly written.

The Fibonacci Series
and the Golden Section:
Comprehension Quiz
Answer Key

1. What is one unique feature of the Fibonacci series?

   There are several possible answers to this question, including that summing the squares of successive Fibonacci numbers will yield another Fibonacci number, that dividing a larger Fibonacci by a smaller will equal phi, that adding all Fibonacci numbers up to one point and then adding 1 will equal the next number in the series, and any mention of the connections between Fibonacci numbers and the natural world.

2. Using a diagram and written captions, explain how the Fibonacci series can be represented on a grid and transformed into an equiangular spiral.

   The diagram should show the grid and the progressively larger squares, with dimensions equal to the Fibonacci series. The latter should be explained. Each square should have an arc joining the corners.

3. List three examples of equiangular spirals in the natural world.

   Any example mentioned in class, or any new and correct example, is acceptable.

4. Explain how pinecones are "designed" around the Fibonacci series.

   Students should explain that the opposing rows of bracts are adjacent Fibonacci numbers. The bracts also spiral like an equiangular spiral.

5. Fill in the missing Fibonacci numbers in the following sequence:

   8, _____, 21, _____, 55, _____, 144
   The missing numbers are 13, 34, and 89.

6. Use two numbers in the series above to create phi. Show your work.

   Students should divide any larger number by an adjacent smaller number.

7. Assume that line segment AC, shown below, is a Golden Section. Circle any of the statements that are true.

   Starred responses are correct.

   * BC ÷ AB = ϕ.

     AB ÷ BC = ϕ.

   * AC ÷ BC = 1.61 . . .

   * The ratio of AB to BC is equal to the ratio of BC to AC.

   If BC is divided in half, it can be used to make a Golden Rectangle.

   * If BC is divided by 1.61, it will equal (approximately) AB.

   * The dimensions of AB and BC can be used to make a Golden Rectangle.

8. Why is phi an irrational number? __c__
   a) Because ϕ has the same value as π.
   b) Because it must be written as a decimal that repeats the same set of numbers.
   c) Because it cannot be completely expressed as a ratio.
   d) Because it is not related to the Golden Section.

9. Given what you now know about the Fibonacci series, the Golden Section, phi, and the Golden Rectangle, complete the sentence below. You may write a paragraph if you wish.

   Math is like . . .
   Here, look for an analogy or simile that explains how mathematics may model the natural world, how we are hardwired to understand math, or perhaps how math serves as a blueprint for theories and art. Answers should display consideration of how mathematics may be more than simply counting or measurement.

Fibonacci Yard Art
Grading Criteria

When assessing students' yard art plans, look for the following elements:

- ⚙ complete plans;

- ⚙ a diagram (or diagrams) with dimensions;

- ⚙ a sensible, step-by-step process; and

- ⚙ calculations (work should be shown, and students may need to recopy their initial calculations, placing them in a coherent, neat order).

Students can also be evaluated for how well they worked together to create the plan. Some standards that apply to this process may include the following:

- ⚙ respectful interaction,

- ⚙ equitable assignment of tasks, and

- ⚙ productive time spent on task.

The students' final plan should be plausible and should involve simple, accessible materials. Students have to understand the interaction of the Fibonacci series and the dimensions of the equiangular spiral in order to plot out a design and the steps needed to complete it. Their plans must demonstrate this, rather than being simply a drawing, without mentioning steps or directions. If you are have time and can secure permission, you might work with your class to paint or draw the spiral of the winning design in an outdoor location.

Reason vs. Revelation

Objectives

⚙ Students will be able to identify and describe the features of the reason vs. revelation dilemma.

⚙ Using their knowledge of reason vs. revelation, students will identify and evaluate current manifestations of this ancient dilemma.

Introduction

In any dispute over weighty matters, one side may challenge the other by asking, "Says who?" It is understood that there must be a source of validation, some authoritative reference. In the opposition of reason vs. revelation, one side is likely to appeal to science or logic, while the other appeals to religion, God, or inexplicable circumstances.

The English word *reason* comes to us, via French, from the Latin *ratio*, meaning a reckoning, calculation, or mental consideration. In contrast, the word *reveal* derives from the Latin noun *velum*, which means veil or covering. Thus, to reveal something is to take the cover off of it, as one would unveil a new monument.

These words' respective roots give us a clear picture of the contrasting ways in which people may seek support for their positions on critical issues. Some will cite scientific experimentation, logical processes, and other mental calculations. Others believe the truth is uncovered through faith, prayer, seeking oracles, or consulting scripture. What is particularly surprising, and even distressing, is the degree to which both sides of the reason vs. revelation opposition fail to recognize each other's fundamental assumptions. Each side interprets the behavior of the other through the lens of its own belief system. For example, in a debate over the teaching of creationism in schools, a devout Christian may question why a science teacher seems unwilling to accept the authority of the Biblical account of creation. The devout believer may decide that the teacher lacks religious faith. Likewise, the teacher may regard the creationist as ignorant and question that person's knowledge of science. Both sides continue to clash over the issue, failing to realize that their disagreement is a symptom of their competing assumptions about how people arrive at the truth. Thinking—or worse, calling—each other godless or ignorant will never solve this rift.

The conflict between reason and revelation has produced some historically significant contests. The growth of secular society and science, beginning in the late Middle Ages, fueled this dispute. Two of the most significant collisions between these opposing worldviews were the legendary prosecution of Galileo by Church authorities in 1633, and the celebrated Scopes trial of 1925. The fact that these two events were separated by almost 300 years testifies to the pervasiveness of the conflict between the mutually exclusive constructs of reason and revelation.

Of course, history is always a bit more complicated. Galileo actually enjoyed the blessing of Church authorities for a good deal of his career. He dedicated his initial work supporting Copernicus's heliocentric theory to Pope Paul III. In spite of this, and perhaps due to Galileo's scathing treatment of his foes, the astronomer found himself at odds with the Vatican in the 1630s. The political landscape had changed under Galileo's feet while he was looking at the heavens. The Inquisition had mounted campaigns against perceived heresies within the Church while Galileo was making florid statements about discoveries that ran contrary to Scripture. Pope Urban and the inquisitors forced Galileo to recant and put him under house arrest, where he remained for the rest of his life.

The effects of the Scopes trial are still seen in classrooms today. A young teacher from Tennessee named John Scopes was prosecuted for teaching about evolution. Clarence Darrow, a celebrated trial attorney

and avowed agnostic, defended Scopes. William Jennings Bryan, a nationally renowned politician and orator, prosecuted Scopes.

The mutually exclusive nature of the competing constructs of reason and revelation are perfectly illustrated by an interesting feature of the Scopes trial. The judge refused to allow Darrow to bring scientists to the stand, yet Bryan was permitted to cite the Bible. The trial had to be conducted within the confines of Scriptural interpretation and state law. As a result, Darrow actually called Bryan to the stand as a Biblical expert!

The clash between reason and revelation may be found everywhere in our modern world. Clearly, the most tragic manifestation of this historic clash of philosophies is terrorism. No reasonable person would claim that terrorists are a valid example of a religious attitude—rather, terrorists take religion and use it as a basis for extreme views and actions. Regardless, it is the secular, scientific nature of Western society that many religious extremists of all faiths find threatening. Some choose to flee; others choose to kill indiscriminately.

The discussion starters and exercises in this chapter are designed to encourage students to consider how the ongoing clash between reason and revelation influences us today. A discussion starter about the Big Bang will ask students to consider how these philosophical views interact. As always, the goal is not to convince students to adhere to one side or the other. Instead, the goal is for them to understand more fully, to think more carefully, and consequently, to behave more civilly.

Most people use the term *theory* rather loosely—and sometimes dismissively. For the purposes of discussions in this book, it is important to consider what a theory really is. A theory is an organized explanation about any phenomenon, always subject to testing and modification as new data emerge. Theories usually include related propositions, and like fishnets, they will often contain disparate phenomena within a single framework. As a matter of fact, the more disparate phenomena that are conclusively embraced by a theory, the stronger is that theory's potential. The aim of science is the systematic interconnection of facts; isolated propositions are not a science, but only the building blocks of one (Cohen & Nagel, 1976).

It is interesting to note that Galileo's evidence for the orbit of planets around the sun was incontrovertible and corroborated by a number of observations and calculations. Today, as he and others did then, we accept the heliocentric view of our solar system as fact. However, when he was prosecuted by the Church and forced to recant, he had to characterize his discoveries as a mere hypothesis. In other words, the sun's central role in the solar system was dismissed as "just a theory."

In a world in which knowledge is tested and expands each day, the-ories that have been confirmed by multiple sources of evidence often serve as our most reliable guides. The ultimate source of truth about a theory is, of course, us. People either advance or reject a theory based on observation and experimentation. This does not offer the same sense of confidence and security as that of revealed knowledge. As a result, the tension between reason and revelation remains as we humans continue to grope about for infallible knowledge.

Classroom Activities and Assessments

The Big Bang Debate (pp. 110–112) is a short scene that may be read or acted by students in order to stimulate discussion. The questions that follow the script can be assigned for homework, writing exercises, or whole- or small-group discussion sections. Remind students that this debate is for purposes of discussion. Although the debate deals with controversial issues—and features characters who espouse one view over another—it is not intended to promote one view over another, or to disrespect any point of view, religion, tradition, culture, and so forth. **When Secularism Moves Into the Neighborhood** (pp. 113–115; answer key on p. 119) is a brief student reading assignment that will allow students to gain an understanding of the historic trend of secularism and its clash with religious and cultural traditions. Following this reading are two assessments, one for **vocabulary** (p. 116) and one for **comprehension** (p. 117). Students can choose from a **menu** (p. 118) of two assignments: They may either research a current debate involving reason vs. revelation (grading criteria provided on p. 120), or they may assume the role of a journalist and write a news report or scripted interview about a famous historic clash between reason and revelation (grading guidelines provided on p. 121). Although grading guidelines are provided for these assignments, it will be up to you whether to grade these activities and how to allocate points.

The Big Bang Debate

Characters: Father Abelard (teacher), Emma, Ethan, Erika, Isaiah, and Courtney (high school students)
Scene: Classroom in St. Ignatius High School

Father Abelard: *(turns on lights after film on Genesis)* Let there be light!

Emma: Ex nihilo!

Abelard: I'm impressed, Emma. "Out of nothing"—right?

Emma: Yeah, if you can believe that.

Abelard: Why not?

Ethan: But why should we? We just talked about the Big Bang in physics last week.

Abelard: Did Mr. Wilson mention anything about light?

Ethan: Yeah, he did. But he also talked about cosmic black something . . .

Erika: Cosmic microwave background radiation.

Abelard: Right. From what I can understand, it is kind of like a fossil of the Big Bang. Actually, it is what remained after the universe started to form atoms, maybe 400,000 years after the Big Bang.

Ethan: That's evidence.

Abelard: What do you mean by "evidence"?

Ethan: Ah . . . something that proves something else, like data or information you find to support your arguments.

Abelard: OK, close enough. However, someone might also say that the creation story in the Bible is evidence, too.

Ethan: But that's not evidence.

Abelard: Why?

Ethan: It's not like the kind of evidence a scientist gets from experiments or something.

Abelard: You do see I'm wearing a clerical collar, right? *(students laugh)*

Ethan: Well, yeah, but . . .

Abelard: Kidding aside, what do you think is the difference between cosmic microwave background radiation and the light mentioned in the Biblical creation story?

Erika: Microwaves aren't light.

Abelard: They could be, though, right? I mean, all you have to do is be able to see a certain spectrum or wavelength of energy and you could call it light. We can't see microwaves, but maybe other creatures can.

Isaiah: You can measure microwave radiation. They can actually hear it as static on some instruments. You can't measure the creation story in the Bible, and nobody actually heard God say, "Let there be light."

Abelard: OK, so scientific evidence can be observed and measured. What else? What are some other differences?

Courtney: Scientists say the energy from the Big Bang kind of cooled down and formed clumps. It formed gasses, stars, and then matter. It sort of fits together.

Abelard: What fits together?

Courtney: The cosmic background microwave radiation explains other things—the evidence fits with other explanations, like how galaxies are in certain formations.

Abelard: The word we use is "corroborate." When new evidence supports existing evidence we have, we say that the new information corroborates the existing evidence. Solid theories will be able to gather lots of independent observations and pieces of evidence that corroborate each other, just like when Sherlock Holmes comes up with lots of evidence that points to the guilty criminal. Does the Big Bang theory have other evidence that corroborates the cosmic microwave background radiation?

Emma: Yeah, we learned that the universe is expanding—not just the galaxies and everything, but that the actual space is expanding and kind of carrying everything along with it.

Abelard: Right. So this points to some point of origin, and an expanding and cooling process. Without getting too technical, it's kind of like the original pudding is cooling down and losing its initial hot energy.

Erika: But you said God's creation of the world could be a theory, couldn't it? We can see that things were created, and we observe light, darkness, oceans, and animals, and we have the Bible as evidence of what God said.

Abelard: We observe all of those things, but is the Bible evidence?

Erika: Sure, it is God's Word.

Abelard: I know what you mean, but for the sake of the others, define "God's Word."

Erika: The Bible was written by people who were in communication with God or inspired by God. So it actually contains the words that God wanted us to hear. It must be evidence.

Isaiah: But that's a different kind of evidence. You have to believe in God, or believe the person God spoke with, before you will take that as any evidence. That's all backwards, because evidence should lead you to believe something. You can't just believe something and *then* look for evidence.

Abelard: Good point. Erika, how would you respond?

Questions:

1. What will Erika probably say?

2. How would you define "evidence"?

3. How does the evidence about cosmic background microwave radiation differ from passages in Genesis?

4. What is Isaiah trying to say? Do you agree with him? Why or why not?

5. Is there a difference between a belief and a theory?

6. What are the differences between evidence, proof, and faith?

When Secularism Moves Into the Neighborhood

Read the following passage, paying attention to the words in bold and how they are used.

Imagine an unusual sacred place, a hybrid of a theme park and a **pilgrimage** site containing shrines from every major religion. Aside from statues, gardens, and shrines, the grounds contain mosques, temples, and other places of worship. Religious schools, halls where theologians debate, courts for settling disputes according to scriptural laws, stone buildings sheltering faith healers, and sacred springs are scattered throughout the property.

Now imagine that this **ecumenical**, multicultural "pilgrimage park" is in the process of being bulldozed to make room for a major research university. The shrines and churches are being torn down and replaced by libraries and laboratories. A law school and medical facility will stand where the courts and halls for theologians once stood. The sacred springs will be used as cooling mechanisms in the university's power plant.

How difficult is it to envision a worldwide protest among the faithful? Clearly, thousands of people would be offended about having their pilgrimage site replaced by the university.

Although the pilgrimage park is not a real location, it has nonetheless existed in hundreds of thousands of *individual* locations, all **revered** by millions of faithful people from diverse cultures throughout history. Like in our scenario, the religious landscape has been—and continues to be—bulldozed to make room for a more secular worldview. Furthermore, the reaction to **secularism** has literally shaped history; at different times, this reaction has been either peaceful or bloody, and either liberating or oppressive. Recent terrorist attacks are yet another (very extreme) response to the march of secularism.

What is *secularism*? It is defined as a shift in which religiously inspired beliefs and attitudes are replaced by nonreligious, often scientific, views. In the culture and traditions of Western societies, secularism has flourished since the **Enlightenment**. Secular, or nonreligious, ideas have

replaced religious doctrine or beliefs in most areas of government, law, education, social policy, and medicine. The same has been true for many parts of the East. In revolutionary China, a Marxist **regime** attempted to create a completely secular society.

As parts of the **developing world**, including many areas of the Middle East, are brought into contact with the growing world economy, secularism rides in on the coattails of Western products, corporations, and banks. People must then negotiate a confusing clash of cultures and beliefs as well as the economic chaos brought about as local markets give way to international ones.

Perhaps none of the ideas or information shared in the previous paragraphs is particularly new or noteworthy for some readers. Regardless, it is important to remember that the Enlightenment, which began more than 400 years ago, is still happening. Its presence is felt everywhere: among teachers as they tell students about the Earth's history, in laboratories dealing with stem cells, in boardrooms of businesses expanding into developing countries, and within our own minds as we balance faith and science.

The framers of the United States Constitution envisioned a secular state free from Church control. Like many of the educated elite of their time, they were deists, believing in a creator God, yet unsure of the details of this God. It is worthwhile to ponder whether they supported freedom *of* religion as a means of fostering freedom *from* religion.

The tensions our founders felt between the competing worlds of faith and secularism reverberate throughout all of our country's major institutions. Interestingly, organized religion within the United States remains vibrant and intact. Tensions may come with tolerance, but the secular nature of our government is not eroding personal belief.

> **The tensions our founders felt between the competing worlds of faith and secularism reverberate throughout all of our country's major institutions.**

Time will tell if other areas of the world can embrace secularism without the bloody battles and intellectual **repression** that characterized so much of European history after the Enlightenment. Right now, it appears that the Middle East and parts of Africa are in the throes of a similar Enlightenment. Unfortunately for citizens of these regions, the best intellectual traditions of the Enlightenment are entwined with legitimate fears of Western exploitation and fresh memories of **imperialism**. As history attests, in the international arena, "enlightened" countries have often behaved in unenlightened fashions.

In some ways, it is tempting (somewhat ironically) to say a prayer for the continued growth of secularism. Some of the most "moral" forms of law and governance, such as the concern for human rights, emerged from the works of Enlightenment figures such as Jean-Jacques Rousseau and John Locke. Furthermore, humans have largely (although not entirely) benefited from advances in science and technology. Whatever the outcome, the shockwaves from the Enlightenment still rattle our planet. We can only hope that the liberties and ideals of this historic era will be embraced in a manner that provides more benefits than threats to future generations everywhere.

Name: _____ Date: _____

When Secularism Moves Into the Neighborhood: Vocabulary

Using extra paper if needed, complete the table below.

Term in Bold	Meaning From Context Clues	Dictionary Definition of Term
List each bolded term used in the passage.	Provide your own meaning or synonym of the word based on what it seems to mean in the passage. Back up your definition with evidence!	Find the primary definition of the word in a standard dictionary and write it below.

When Secularism Moves Into the Neighborhood: Comprehension

Using extra paper if needed, answer the questions below.

1. According to the author, what historical event is still going on? Is the author convincing? Explain your answer.

   _____

   _____

   _____

   _____

2. Describe two other examples (not mentioned in the passage) of the clash between secularism and traditions from earlier religious times or cultures.

   _____

   _____

   _____

   _____

3. The author makes some claims about secularism in the developing world—what are they?

   _____

   _____

   _____

   _____

4. Why would a prayer for secularism be ironic? Do you believe the author is correct in making this final conclusion?

   _____

   _____

   _____

   _____

Assignment Menu

Assignment 1: Where else does the reason vs. revelation conflict show up? Research a current debate that involves a clash between reason and revelation. Create a PowerPoint presentation or poster on the issue. The presentation or poster should have the following headings and content:

- ⚙ **Issue:** Write a one-paragraph summary of the topic and debate.

- ⚙ **Point and Counterpoint:** Create a chart with the topic at the top above two columns. The one on the left should list four important arguments supporting one side of the topic, and the column on the right should list four important counterarguments.

- ⚙ **Current Status:** What is the current status of the debate? Have laws been passed? Have citizens been surveyed or polled on the topic?

- ⚙ **Where You Stand:** What is your position on this debate? What are your reasons (or revelations)?

Possible topics to explore for this assignment include the Scopes trial, the Shroud of Turin, stem cell research, teaching evolution and creationism in public schools, faith healing, and beliefs about the end of the world.

Assignment 2: Be a news anchor. Research a famous historic clash between reason and revelation. Write a script for a news report, and interview one or more of the historic figures involved. For instance, if your news report were on the Scopes trial, you would cover the circumstances surrounding the trial and interview William Jennings Bryan and Clarence Darrow.

When Secularism Moves Into the Neighborhood

Answer Key

Vocabulary Chart

Grading this chart is fairly subjective; the student should have provided definitions of each term, along with explanations from the context of the passage to support the given definitions. For the dictionary definitions, the student should have given the primary definition of each term.

Comprehension Questions

1. According to the author, what historical event is still going on? Is the author convincing? *The Enlightenment is still affecting us. Any response to the additional question is acceptable as long as students support their answers.*

2. Describe two other examples (not mentioned in the passage) of the clash between secularism and religious or cultural traditions. *Examples include religious opposition to medical procedures, debates over creationism, clashes over homosexuality and gay marriage, opposition to polygamy, birth control, opposition to genetically modified crops, and cloning; students may think of additional examples.*

3. The author makes some claims about secularism in the developing world—what are they? *The author claims that Western corporations, products, and banks also add to the confusion.*

4. Why would a prayer for secularism be ironic? Do you believe the author is correct in making this final conclusion? *A prayer for secularism would be ironic because a secular worldview does not include prayer. Students' positions agreeing or disagreeing with the author should be supported with reasoning.*

Name:_____ Date:_____

Assignment 1
Grading Criteria

Headings: Absent _____ points **Partially Complete** _____ points **Complete** _____ points

List of Sources: Absent _____ points **Present** _____ points

	Poor	Adequate	Good	Superior
Comprehension				
Organization				
Neatness, appearance				
Usage, mechanics				
Other				

Comments:

_____

_____

_____

Total Points: _____ out of _____ possible

Assignment 2

Grading Guidelines

Points should be assigned for the following criteria:

1. Student prepares a script with clearly written or typed dialogue.

2. Student gives an accurate report of a clash or controversy.

3. Student's project is an appropriate length and format for a news feature.

4. Student demonstrates comprehension of important points.

5. Student lists sources.

CHAPTER

8

Free Will vs. Determinism

Objectives

⚙ Students will identify modern versions of the ancient questions about human freedom and destiny.

⚙ Students will assess the implications of belief in both free will and determinism.

⚙ Students will comprehend how decisions about free will and determinism affect our appraisal of human behavior.

Introduction

Two cows are standing in a pasture. One says to the other, "What do you think about this mad cow disease?"
"What do I care?" replies the other cow. "I'm a helicopter!"

This bizarre little joke illustrates a very important point about existence. All of us (especially cows) are constrained by reality. We live in a world in which we seem to have little control over many of the basic features of our lives. Try as we might, there's no way we can wish ourselves into being helicopters.

Obviously, we are not utterly free to be anything we wish. Our minds may will something, but the physical state of our world will control, and often thwart, our desires. We look around us and see the inevitable laws of cause and effect and the predictable patterns of the stars, planets, and seasons. Although they may possess volition, animals are nonetheless regulated by instinct. Frogs croak every spring, swallows catch insects, geese migrate, and salmon spawn in the home headwaters. None of them seem to ask why, or whether there is a better way of doing things. Humans seem to be alone in struggling against the bonds of our material world. So how free are we?

The following chapter, a survey of the perennial debate between free will and determinism, is not intended to be comprehensive. Scores of thinkers and generations of brilliant philosophers will be ignored, while others will be recognized only in passing. The topic is too pervasive, too ingrained within our existence, to be adequately treated by a single work, let alone a single chapter. The opposition of free will and determinism qualifies as a foundation of Western thought.

Questions of freedom and fate arguably helped give rise to religion (Hopfe, 1994), a phenomenon found in all cultures. Whole societies, from the Sumerians to modern-day tribes, have regarded human beings as creatures at the mercy of an assortment of capricious gods. Both creation stories in the Bible's book of Genesis specify the subordinate position of humans within God's grand design. Indeed, Adam and Eve were punished for exercising too much freedom.

Aristotle referred to God as the "unmoved mover," a moniker that characterizes God as the "first cause" of all else that happened in the universe, whereas Aristotle's teacher, Plato, referred to God as the "self-moving mover" (Jones, 1970). Neither assumed that cause and effect could be eternal. Instead, they proposed that something had to have brought the hurly-burly events of our world into being.

Plato and Aristotle believed that the world, set in motion, was changing towards a particular end state. In other words, that things happen because there is a purpose. However, Plato believed that the blueprint for the end state of the universe was located in a transcendent world consisting of ideal forms for everything we see. For Aristotle, this same blueprint was present in our world, with a plan located within each object, driving that object towards its final goal. Oddly, his view of cause and effect included an object's inherent purpose as one of four causal factors. Today, not many people would say that a wave rolls to shore because it

is fulfilling its essential purpose. However, Aristotle would defend this notion.

Regardless of the two men's beliefs about the purpose of the endless chain of cause and effect, neither left much room for random events or human freedom. Plato warned us to act in accordance with divine purpose, and Aristotle warned us to act in accordance with individual purpose.

From the 4th–16th centuries, Christian theologians and scholars such as Augustine, Boethius, Aquinas, Luther, Calvin, and Erasmus all wrestled with the concepts of free will and determinism. For them, the language varied, but the concepts (inherited from Saint Paul's emphasis on the "fall of man") were the same. The central questions focused on original sin, God's control and foreknowledge of all that happens, and our ability to attain salvation through repentance and good works. A complicating factor for all of these scholars, especially during the days of the Reformation, involved the conflict between predestination and God's grace. The reasoning went something like this: If God foreordains everything, then God certainly knows who is to be saved and who is to be condemned. If this is true, then it has all been decided already—so why strive to be virtuous? You will either be among the "elect," or you will be doomed.

But before you accept that argument and yield to temptation, recall that a lot of scholarly ink has been spilled in favor of good works and the ultimate reward of salvation. However, good works alone cannot control God. So where does all of the theological hand wringing leave us? Some ministers, scholars, and believers may give you the brushoff regarding the conundrum. If they think about it at all, most Christians simply shrug their shoulders and hedge their bets by upholding faith *and* practicing good works.

The debates among religious thinkers were intricate, fascinating, and occasionally tedious, even to students of religious thought. Nevertheless, they brought us closer to understanding the psychological nature of the free will vs. determinism duality.

Modern debates over free will and determinism are still deeply psychological in nature. They have to do with our motivations and what controls our actions. Beginning with Sigmund Freud (1856–1939), a determinist, modern people became intrigued with the causes of human behavior, especially those behaviors and emotions that may seem unusual or deviant. Today, courts routinely summon psychologists to testify both on behalf of and against defendants. Therapists help us gain control over emotions or behaviors we may previously have considered uncontrollable. Television and popular publications introduce us to scores of psychologists, therapists, and other experts (some actually experts, and others phonies) who claim the capacity to harness some causal law of human behavior and effectively twist it to help us.

One of the greatest debates in psychology occurred in the middle of the 20th century between behaviorists and humanists. Behaviorists were determinists and regarded outward behavior as the only useful variable worth studying. Humanists, on the other hand, were more likely to promote free will, and insisted that any science of human behavior had to take emotion and volition into account.

One behaviorist in particular, B. F. Skinner (1904–1990), improved the standard model of behaviorism to be far more methodologically fruitful and potentially threatening to those who espouse free choice. Expanding on his ideas, he wrote a controversial utopian novel about a reclusive community that used behavioral engineering to achieve happiness for all in the society (Skinner, 1975). Classical behaviorists like Ivan Pavlov (1849–1936) had already postulated that creatures were controlled by various environmental stimuli. Although Skinner didn't question this, his theory was richer and provided a more detailed explanation. Skinner's "organisms" (a term he used even for humans) acted in ways that could have rewarding (positive), aversive (negative), or neutral consequences. Whether an action yielded rewarding, aversive, or neutral consequences would reinforce or inhibit future behavior. After a while, the organism would engage in whatever behavior produced the desired consequence. Thus, Skinner believed that behavior is shaped by the *interaction* of the organism and the environment, but that the environment ultimately controls the organism via consequences.

One could argue that within Skinner's belief system, an organism is most free while at rest. The moment that organism acts, the environment either rewards or punishes that action in such a way that in the future, that action will change (or remain the same) in order to produce the most rewarding results. This makes behavior less random and more predictable. Of course, even being at rest is a choice, an action with consequences. If an organism behaves in a predictable way—to avoid negative consequences and seek reward—is that organism more purposeful?

Skinner insisted that words such as *purpose* and *intent* do not refer to measurable, observable states. What we call intent, he would argue, is nothing more than a conditioned response to environmental contingencies. Skinner thought that as the science of behavior progressed, words such as intent and freedom would become less meaningful and valid. In a polemical work entitled *Beyond Freedom and Dignity*, Skinner (1972)

stated, "Autonomous man is a device used to explain what we cannot explain in any other way" (p. 191).

Skinner did not doubt that we often *feel* free, but he argued this is an internal, unobservable state. He argued that these subjective feelings—and the words we are taught to attach to them—are cultural products. Skinner (1971) believed that even consciousness itself was a social product that could not exist if we were literally reared in isolation—that is, hypothetically, a human being raised by wolves would not develop individual consciousness, but would think like a wolf.

A host of psychologists, philosophers, and writers have argued against the rigidly deterministic views of people like Skinner. Since the Enlightenment in the 17th and 18th centuries, these individuals have attempted to liberate humans from tyrants including a wrathful God, the laws of physics, the control of society, the limitations of the human brain, the control of powerful social classes, the narrow confines of organized religion, and the clutches of scientific reductionism.

In all cases, these thinkers have proposed that there is something special about humans, something that enables us to transcend the limitations of our physical and social existence. They assert that regardless of our circumstances, we often feel free to make choices. We may not like the choices we are offered or the consequences we experience, but our reactions are based on the fact that we sense our capacity to be free. Without this sense, we would be as satisfied as fish in a tank, never challenging our boundaries.

For existentialists, romantics, and humanists, people are capable of determining how they respond to their environments. In the latter part of the 20th century, this thinking gave rise to the human potential movement, a school of thought in psychology that stressed our ability to gain self-knowledge and to experience fuller, more authentic lives. The ideas expressed by scores of writers such as Erich Fromm, Carl Rogers, and Abraham Maslow contrasted with Skinner's narrowly scientific worldview. Although this conflict subsided, the tensions remain.

In this chapter, students can investigate whether they feel free. Is this feeling of freedom only subjectively experienced, or is it objectively true? What happens to our moral standards, or to those qualities that we value (e.g., heroism, justice, self-sacrifice) if we are not free? These are fascinating questions to explore. The lessons and exercises in this chapter will direct students' attention to one of the greatest oppositions in the history of Western thought.

Classroom Activities and Assessments

The Courageous Firefighter (pp. 129–133; journal/discussion questions on p. 134) is a short story designed to elicit student conversation about a troubling aspect of determinism. Although many people are quick to recognize that the absence of choice means that people cannot be blamed for their actions, it is often more distressing to realize that the absence of choice would also mean that people cannot really take credit or praise for worthwhile actions. The questions following the story can be used for discussion, journal entries, or grading purposes. **Defining Free Choice** (pp. 136–137) contains questions that may be used either to foster classroom discussion or as journal responses. **A Future World** (pp. 138–139; journal/discussion questions on p. 140) may be read aloud to students or copied for them to read individually or in groups. It presents a scenario that prompts students to consider what it would be like to live in a world where risks were controlled and happiness was guaranteed in exchange for the loss of freedom. Again, this activity can be used to foster whole- or small-group discussion, or you can copy it and use it as a journal or writing assignment prompt. The provided **Evaluation Criteria for Written Responses** (p. 141) can be used to consider students' responses.

The Courageous Firefighter

On a blustery day in November, in the middle of another algebra quiz, our school caught on fire. Like most of my classmates, I thought it was a fire drill when we first filed out of the building. However, when all of us saw the smoke billowing out of the gym, we fell silent. After a while, some students started to panic. Unsure of what to do with all of the adrenaline in their systems, some simply jumped up and down, pointing and yelling. A few reached for their cell phones and took pictures.

Administrators and teachers herded the crowd towards the muddy edges of the parking area. Soon we could hear sirens in the distance. A ladder truck and two others pulled up beside the gym. Seconds later, an ambulance parked near the side of the building. I couldn't believe how fast those people moved. Within minutes, the ladder was extended and a firefighter had clambered up, grabbing the nozzle and planting herself above the smoking gymnasium. Several more firefighters placed themselves around the building with hoses, and two ran towards the gym doors.

A firefighter sprinted over to us and yelled through a bullhorn. "Is everyone out of the building?" Teachers looked at their clipboards and shouted names. Students raised their hands or shouted back. Suddenly, Ms. Keller gasped. "Where's Mr. Eubanks?" she asked. Mr. Eubanks was a popular gym teacher and basketball coach—everyone liked him. After the administrators and several students called his name and looked around the crowd, they announced that he was missing.

"I thought I saw him in the locker room when I left," offered one student. "He was holding a fire extinguisher."

The firefighter radioed to two others at the gym doors. One broke the doors open with a large hatchet, and they both went in. They were wearing special equipment and oxygen masks.

We could feel the heat of the fire, even at a distance of more than a football field.

The fire raged and flames licked the sky. We could feel the heat of the fire, even at a distance of more than a football field. The firefighters had to pull the ladder truck back. I could see them running around and yelling at one another. The captain motioned frantically to the ambulance driver. Two other firefighters went in through the gym doors and came out carrying one of the firefighters who had gone in after Mr. Eubanks—he was unconscious, but the other firefighter and Mr. Eubanks were still in the school.

We all waited, holding our breath and looking for any sign of them. It was then that the roof and one side wall caved in. It was as if the bricks had simply melted. Fortunately, they had just moved the truck out of the way—otherwise, more people could have been killed.

It began to dawn on us that Mr. Eubanks and the firefighter might not get out alive. Some students and teachers were crying. We couldn't quite believe what we were seeing.

Our worst fears turned out to come true. Mr. Eubanks was killed when the roof collapsed, and so was one of the firefighters who had tried to save him. Mr. Eubanks's funeral was held out of state because his elderly mother could not travel. A few administrators and teachers went to the service, and the school planned a separate memorial service. Counselors were brought in to help students and teachers deal with their grief.

However, about 50 of us went to the funeral for the firefighter who tried to save Mr. Eubanks. His name was Montell Daniels. The story was covered on the national news. People from the *Tomorrow Show* interviewed his widow. He was a hero.

After the funeral, I offered Bradley Renniks a ride back to school. It was snowing, and he didn't have a car. Renniks is a really smart guy, but sometimes he says things before he really thinks. Actually, the real problem is that he sometimes says troubling things—things that other people wouldn't say. Sometimes it would be better if he kept his thoughts to himself, or at least waited until a more appropriate time, but I guess if he did that, then he wouldn't be Renniks.

As I was pulling out of the church parking lot, Renniks said, "What did you think of the eulogy that the fire chief gave?"

The fire chief had called Montell Daniels a genuine hero, someone who put his own life ahead of others' lives. I thought it was inspiring. We've all read those kinds of things before, and heard those kinds of speeches—in the movies, or in the news. However, I had actually seen Montell Daniels and his fellow firefighter go into the burning building. It must have been a nightmare in there. "I thought he did a good job," I replied. "He was obviously choked up—Daniels was a brave guy."

"Look, no disrespect here," said Renniks, holding up his hands. "But I don't think there are any real heroes."

"Why not?" I asked.

"Because a guy like Daniels is just going to do what he was trained to do. I mean, a firefighter couldn't refuse to go into a burning building, could he? He'd be fired from his job."

"Yeah," I countered, "but he could have turned around when he got to the gymnasium and saw how dangerous it was in there. He radioed for help when his partner collapsed, but he didn't run out."

"Of course not," said Renniks. "He wouldn't have been able to live with himself, wondering if he could have saved Eubanks. The guilt would have been too much. Besides, if he'd rescued Eubanks and gotten out alive, then he would have been honored for being a hero."

"Dude," I yelled, "how can you be so cold?"

"I'm not cold. Don't get me wrong—I'm not saying I could ever do what Daniels did. But let's face it, the fact remains that he would have been honored for being a hero if he'd saved Eubanks."

"He was called a hero today," I said.

"Right," Renniks said. "And so you could say that either way, he knew he'd be a hero."

"Are you saying Daniels was selfish?" I was angry and felt sick about what Renniks was saying, but I couldn't change the subject—I wanted to convince him.

"No, this is different," Renniks said. "He gave up his whole life, and he'll never see his wife again. Of course he's not selfish. But he was just doing what he was conditioned to do."

"You make it sound like someone *trained* him to sacrifice himself, like a guard dog," I said.

"They did," answered Renniks. "Actually, *we* did. You know, if we didn't offer honor and heroism to people like Daniels, then all of us would be in greater danger. Instead, we offer awards and honor to soldiers, police officers, firefighters, and other people we ask to protect us."

"But you make it sound like there's nothing special about it," I protested, "like it's disrespectful or undignified or something."

I was getting pretty angry with Renniks, and I was also really thirsty. I pulled into a convenience store so I could gather myself, grab a drink, and cool down. I hoped that Renniks would get the picture and shut up.

"Look," said Renniks. "I don't like my ideas any more than you do. I'm just being honest, that's all. Only a suicidal person would willingly end his life. Daniels wasn't suicidal, obviously. He was just responding to the way he had been trained all of his life—not just at the fire station."

"A parent would die for his or her child," I offered.

> Only a suicidal person would willingly end his life. Daniels wasn't suicidal, obviously. He was just responding to the way he had been trained all of his life . . .

"Yeah," said Renniks. "But say a mother died for her child—she'd be doing it for a lot of the same reasons. She wouldn't be able to live with grief if her child died, and she would also want her genes to live on. She would still be working for the best possible outcome."

"Man, you are full of it." I sighed. "Let's just let it rest for awhile and get something to drink."

We walked into the store. My shoes chirped on the sticky tile floor. As I made my way over to the coolers to look over the beverages, I could see Renniks glancing at some cookies near the register. I grabbed a large plastic bottle of green tea and headed for the cashier. Renniks finally selected his cookie and lined up behind me.

Back in the car, Renniks took a bite out of his cookie and turned to me, cupping his hands under his chin to catch a falling crumb. "So, why did you choose that green tea?" he asked.

I thought it was a weird question, but I was relieved to be done arguing about Daniels. "It's really sweet. It's probably bad for you—it's got tons of corn syrup. But I love corn syrup!" I said.

Renniks chuckled. "So is it sweeter than soda and other drinks?"

"Oh, yeah," I assured him. "It's the sweetest. I'm glad I discovered it." I pulled out of the parking lot and headed up Chalet Street to our school.

"So you didn't just pick any drink—you chose the one that was most rewarding to you, right? I mean, the sweetest and the best tasting."

I was getting suspicious of Renniks's motives now, but I answered him anyway. "Sure. Why would I pick something I hate, like ginger ale?"

"Did you have to drink ginger ale whenever you were sick?" asked Renniks. "I did."

"Yep," I answered.

"OK, so you chose the drink that gave you the most pleasurable thoughts and avoided the one that had the worst associations, like with being sick when you were little. Now, how can you really say that you *chose* your drink?" asked Renniks.

"Because I walked over to the refrigerator and bought it!" I answered. "I would have bought you one, too, if weren't so full of obnoxious questions." I tried to be humorous, but my voice still had a defensive edge to it.

Renniks was unfazed. "So did you *really* make a choice? Wasn't it kind of decided already? You've been trained by your experience to drink sweet green tea. The people who make it put tons of corn syrup in it, and you said yourself that you love corn syrup. How is that free choice?"

"I could have had anything else," I replied.

"But you didn't," he said.

I parked, shut off the ignition, and turned to him. "No, I didn't. But what's the point? You had a white chocolate cookie!"

"Sure, that's my favorite. I'll even admit that I've been trained by experience to like them!" exclaimed Renniks. This wasn't the response I had hoped for.

"Do you want me to admit that I probably wouldn't choose anything other than sweet green tea or something with corn syrup? Fine. Maybe it's in the stars or something," I said.

"It's just a conditioned choice with rewards and consequences," offered Renniks. He paused and then said, "Just like Daniels's choice to try to save Eubanks!"

I groaned. "We'll just have to agree to disagree on that one," I said.

The Courageous Firefighter

Questions

1. After reading the short story, summarize Renniks's points in 1–2 paragraphs.

_____

_____

_____

_____

_____

_____

_____

_____

_____

_____

_____

_____

_____

2. Do you agree or disagree with Renniks? Explain your reasoning.

_____

_____

_____

_____

_____

_____

_____

3. How do Rennicks's comments make you feel? Are they maddening, insightful, or discouraging? Is he mean-spirited, or honest? Why do you think his comments evoke these emotions?

_____

_____

_____

_____

_____

_____

_____

_____

Defining Free Choice

1. Define "freedom." If freedom is the ability to do what you want, are you free, or simply controlled by what you want? If you state that you are free to do what you *don't* want to do, then doesn't this just mean that you want to prove you are free?

   _____

   _____

   _____

   _____

   _____

   _____

   _____

2. According to behaviorists, you have never made a free choice—you have always chosen what is most rewarding to you (or less punishing) at the time. Think of a time that you did something you did not want to do. What was it?

   _____

   _____

   _____

   _____

   _____

   _____

   _____

3. Referring to your answer for the previous question, why did you do something that you did not want to do? Behaviorists would say that you did it because either the consequence would be rewarding or at least less unpleasant than the alternative. Is this true in the case of your example?

   _____

   _____

   _____

   _____

   _____

   _____

   _____

4. If we take determinism seriously, then we cannot be honored for our actions, and neither can we be blamed for our bad choices. Everything we do would be hypothetically beyond our control. Assume that psychologists were able to prove that none of our choices were free. Could you live in such a world? How would it affect you?

_____

_____

_____

_____

_____

_____

_____

5. Assume that scientists were able to prove that some criminals do not choose to commit their crimes, but rather that such behavior is the result of genetics and specific environmental triggers. Would you accept this discovery? Why or why not?

_____

_____

_____

_____

_____

_____

_____

A Future World

Assume that tomorrow night you brush your teeth and go to bed, just as you have for years. The following "morning," you awaken to an obnoxious humming in your ears. You open your eyes and see a man and a woman wearing surgical masks scanning your head with a device that looks like a glowing curling iron. They both turn to look at a screen behind them. It appears to be monitoring your vital signs.

"Where am I?" you ask.

"We weren't sure that we could revive you!" exclaims the man. "How do you feel?"

"My throat is dry," you croak. "Am I at the hospital?"

The man and the woman tell you that you have actually awakened 200 years in the future. The night you brushed your teeth and went to sleep, you went into a coma due to a rare disease you were unaware you had, as you had not demonstrated any symptoms until that point. Your family could not wake you up and sent for an ambulance. You were very close to death, so your family, faced with a very difficult decision, decided to agree to have you cryogenically frozen in a facility that had perfected this process. The technique worked for you and a few others, and you are now celebrities. Because you were perfectly preserved in your frozen state, you have not aged, and you have retained all of your memories from the past.

Naturally, it takes you several months to mourn the loss of your past life and to adjust to the new world in which you find yourself. You remain in the institution where you woke up, where counselors help you. Near the end of this time, the people at the clinic tell you that the world you are about to enter is far safer and more peaceful than the one you knew before. There are no wars, crimes, or personal problems like divorce or alcoholism. Your caretakers tell you that specialists finally mastered and implemented the laws governing human behavior. These laws involve a combination of brain activity, important experiences, and genetics. Now, they inform you, it is absolutely certain that people are not free to make choices. Because scientists know about the choices that people will make, they are able to control the chaos that creates our problems.

On the day you are released from the clinic, you are sent to the State Department of Human Prognostication (SDHP), one of 60 regional government laboratories, where you are given a battery of psychological, neurological, and blood chemistry tests. The scientists working in this laboratory will then develop a Gnosis Profile. This profile will be stored in a database that generates reports any time you have an important decision to make. Specialists have decided to allow people to keep making small "decisions" in order to preserve the illusion of freedom and the mental health that such an idea promotes.

At the end of these tests, you will be assigned a college and a major. When you graduate, the database will guide SDHP counselors in assigning you a job and a marriage partner. You object to this prospect, but experts assure you that these were the choices you would have (or should have) made anyway. Why would you waste time or money on bad choices or indecision?

A Future World

Questions

1. Would you be happy if you lived in this future world? (Remember, there are no mistakes, less heartache, and few failures.) Why or why not?

_____

_____

_____

_____

_____

_____

2. Do you know anyone who once made a bad choice? Would it have helped if that person could have relied on the SDHP database from this future world? Why or why not?

_____

_____

_____

_____

_____

_____

3. We can determine how animals will behave. (For instance, we can train dogs, and we can predict how long rats will attempt to escape from a maze before giving up.) Do you think it will be ever be possible to determine how people will behave?

_____

_____

_____

_____

_____

_____

Evaluation Criteria for Written Responses

Journal and short-essay responses may be evaluated in much the same ways as discussion. Students should present relevant comments that exhibit a reflective attitude and careful thought. If you choose to grade journal responses, consider a scoring method that rates journal entries according to one or several of the following criteria:

- support of statements;
- explanation of reasons and rationale for answers;
- reflection on main ideas and problems;
- making connections with other readings, prior knowledge, or previous class discussions;
- demonstration of creative thinking; and
- discussion of implications.

When dealing with the more subjective responses, it works well to write an example of an ideal answer or to display a student sample, to show students what you are looking for in terms of reflection, evidence, thoughtfulness, and so on. If you do grade written responses, it is best to skim them before going back and assigning grades, as some topics are particularly difficult for students to grasp, or the classroom discussion often leads students to draw similar conclusions. Reading a sample of the responses before assigning grades will give you a better idea of the type of work you will be grading.

CHAPTER 9

Liberalism vs. Conservatism

Objectives

⚙ Students will state at least two essential characteristics of each ideology (conservative and liberal).

⚙ When encountering media coverage of current events, students will categorize stated opinions as mainly liberal or conservative.

⚙ Students will critically evaluate events without relying solely on either liberal or conservative ideology.

Introduction

Conservative, n: A statesman who is enamored of existing evils, as distinguished from the Liberal who wishes to replace them with others.
—Ambrose Bierce

It is perhaps best to begin this chapter with a healthy skepticism towards both liberalism and conservatism, as suggested so wittily by Ambrose Bierce's quote. This chapter, like the other chapters in this book, does not advocate one political view over the next. Rather, the terms *liberal* and *conservative* refer to a deeper disagreement lying at the basic nature of human beings—an insolvable, eternal dichotomy.

These opposing labels have been worn by many different people over the years. The opinions of liberals, as well as the opinions of conservatives, have varied widely and have morphed both over time and within parties. This can make any historical study of the opposing concepts rather confusing.

The source of the word liberal is the Latin adjective *liberalis*, which is derived from *liber*, meaning "free." Related English words are liberty and liberate. It is the basic notion of freedom that influences our past and current understandings of the word and its derivatives.

Throughout the history of political thought in Europe and the Americas, liberals have held a variety of positions and theories, some of them contradictory when examined over a period of time. For our purposes, however, it is safe to ignore this historical complexity and focus on the very general features that distinguish liberalism from conservatism in present-day American politics.

What are the essential liberal tenets found in American political thought? Although this may be earnestly debated by hundreds of well-informed people, we can boil liberalism down to three basic tenets. First, individuals (although not necessarily groups of individuals) possess an inherent goodness and wisdom; second, the freedom of the individual must be protected; and third, any government or other large institution is likely to abuse its power and seek absolute political and economic control of individuals.

Because liberals believe that humans are inherently good, they also believe that individuals should consent to be governed, and that power should be curtailed, lest it interfere with the individual's freedom (O'Neill, 1981). An important liberal answer to the potential threat of an overreaching government is the doctrine of the separation of powers, elaborated in the United States Constitution.

Alert readers will be asking a perceptive question at this point. If it is true that liberal political theory despises government interference with individual freedom, then why do so many so-called liberal policies rely upon large federal and state programs? At the risk of saying too much, this paradox may be attributed to two factors. First, liberals tend to embrace experimental government policies that attempt to support or empower individuals (e.g., welfare, food stamps, childcare initiatives). These programs may support individuals, but they also, by necessity, add to the size and role of government. Second, liberals appear to rely upon their government to protect the individual from the potential dangers of

powerful forces such as corporations, unfair markets, ethnic prejudices, and even their own or other governments (Caporaso & Levine, 1992). In other words, liberals turn to legislation and judicial oversight to curtail power, even within the government.

So what of conservatism? This term comes from Latin as well. Its source is the verb *servare*, meaning "to save, keep, or retain." The prefix *con* (meaning "with") adds force to the word. The word conservative, then, connotes a tendency to hold, keep, hold back, and so on. Conservatives are less likely than liberals are to consider individuals inherently good or wise. For them, society does not necessarily thwart individual freedom. Instead, society and government control our less admirable impulses. We are, according to conservative beliefs, better in groups. Conservatives are more likely to enthusiastically endorse traditional groups and social institutions ranging from organized religion to the Rotary Club.

In his book *The Conservatives: Ideas and Attitudes Throughout American History*, Patrick Allitt (2009) wrote,

> I argue that conservatism is, first of all, an *attitude* to social and political change that looks for support to the ideas, beliefs, and habits of the past and puts more faith in the lessons of history than in the abstractions of political philosophy. (p. 2)

Somewhat less flatteringly, Woodrow Wilson is rumored to have defined a conservative as someone "who makes no changes and consults his grandmother when in doubt."

Although conservatives have faith in the ability of traditional institutions (such as the church or the local chamber of commerce) to regulate the worst of our impulses, they remain paradoxically individualistic when it comes to participation in the economy. The root of this paradox is found in the *free market*. In capitalist systems, the free market is not an actual place so much as it is a theoretical category of places ranging from a bait shop to the Chicago Board of Trade. In an ideal free market, production, distribution, and the exchange of goods and services are controlled solely by private individuals and entities—in other words, not regulated by the government (Hirsch, Kett, & Trefil, 2002). For centuries, the merchant classes of Europe and America fought government control (especially taxation) and enjoyed a jealously guarded tradition of private investment and expansion. Many claim that the merchant class also enjoyed a fair amount of government collusion and self-serving protection. Regardless, this was a traditional, tried-and-true form of economic life, and many wished to conserve it (although the conservative label did not come into use until the late 19th century).

Liberals, led by thinkers such as Karl Marx and Fredrick Engels (the latter was a factory owner), grew to distrust the "freedom" of the free market. Marx saw the free market as a means of exploitation whereby the surplus value of products and services lined the pockets of the elite and served to entrap workers in a powerless position (Engels, 1891). For liberals (and Marxists or socialists), the market needed to be planned and controlled in order to give power back to individuals, who they believed were inherently more worthy of trust than the powerful elite controlling the economy. Thus, liberals grew to trust government control (as opposed to individual autonomy) when it came to operating the market.

The history of Marxism in Russia and China, where it failed, may serve as a vindication for conservative ideologists. However, many proposals by Marxists and early liberals that were originally considered radical, such as minimum wage and ending child labor, are now readily accepted by conservatives and liberals alike. As with all of the oppositions presented in this book, any time people fully embrace one side of the dispute or the other, false doctrines are imposed and certain situations cannot be solved. Perhaps it is most important for liberals and conservatives to uphold their essential precepts and to maintain a healthy dialogue.

Classroom Activities and Assessments

Suggested Questions for Discussion (p. 148) will inspire classroom discussion or journal responses. These questions may be used either to introduce the unit, or as a means of encouraging discussion after the basic concepts have already been presented. **Concept Sorting** (p. 149; key on p. 152) is an activity requiring students to categorize ideas, organizations, policies, and other features of American life as being either essentially liberal or essentially conservative. The activity may be done in small groups or on a whiteboard or other visual display. It may also be used as a worksheet, and you may choose to add items to the list. Students should justify their category choices. **Political Science** (pp. 150–151; rubric on p. 153) gives students an opportunity to conduct research with people, or by surveying the media, to determine the prevalence and extent of conservative and liberal views.

Suggested Questions for Discussion

1. Why are liberals and conservatives called what they are?

2. Are you a liberal or a conservative? Why?

3. Respond to the following quote: "If you're not a liberal at 20, then you have no heart, and if you're not a conservative at 40, then you have no head."

4. Is it possible to have beliefs that fall exactly in between those of liberals and those of conservatives?

5. Rate whether you have a lot of trust, a medium amount of trust, or very little trust in the following: Congress, news stations, schools, churches/mosques/synagogues, your neighborhood, your team or club, older people, younger people, teachers, and law enforcement. How do your rankings relate to the material on liberalism, conservatism, and trust in individuals and groups?

6. Is your family mostly liberal, mostly conservative, or neither? Do liberalism and conservatism "run in families"? Do most people adopt their parents' views and retain them throughout life?

Concept Sorting

Liberal	Conservative

First, decide whether the following concepts and ideas belong on the liberal or the conservative side of the above chart. Write each item in the column where you think it belongs.

Prayer in public schools

Tax breaks for people who buy energy-efficient cars

Government control of industrial waste

Censorship of YouTube

The Boy Scouts

Private charities for poor people instead of state programs

Regulations for landlords

Industries monitoring their own waste

Federal law stating that all new cars will be energy-efficient

Next, circle two items on each side of the chart. Explain in the space below why you placed these items where you did. Apply what you have learned about the characteristics of liberal and conservative thinking, and use extra paper if you need to.

_____

_____

_____

_____

_____

_____

_____

_____

_____

_____

Political Science

It is your turn to be a political scientist. The table below compares modern liberal and conservative viewpoints on a variety of issues and values. After examining the table, you will be asked to design a survey or measurement instrument based on the information in the table and the concepts you have learned.

Issue	Liberal viewpoint	Conservative viewpoint
Human nature	Trusts basic human nature	Distrusts basic human nature
Government power	Assumes that any form of government is likely to abuse its power	Trusts that traditional forms of government are required to make humans behave well
Human differences in achievement	Believes that environment (or nurture) accounts for most differences	Believes that people's innate capacities (nature) and efforts account for most differents
Government's role in individuals' lives	Assumes that some people will need government assistance to achieve equal status or affluence	Assumes that people can improve their status and affluence through individual effort and ability
Role of legislation and policy	Shows willingness to experiment with new initiatives or programs to shape society towards desired ends	Is unwilling to experiment with new initiatives or programs, preferring to maintain and rely upon traditional institutions and individual initiative
Government influence	Favors government influence such as social welfare programs like food stamps, and favors the expansion of public education, environmental regulation, and progressive income tax	Distrusts government influence and favors individual initiatives such as private charity instead of social welfare programs and self-regulation instead of environmental laws; favors regressive income tax and an overall reduction in programs
Military	Distrusts the military and favors diplomacy and treaties	Favors the military and is less trusting of diplomacy and treaties
Labor	Favors unions and the general protection of labor, such as with minimum wages and extensions of benefits	Is generally opposed to unions, believing that workers benefit when companies can compete rather than negotiating
Social issues	Opposes capital punishment and favors individual choice (e.g., supports gay marriage, supports abortion rights)	Favors capital punishment, and believes that traditional customs and laws take precedence over individual choice (e.g., is opposed to gay marriage)

After studying the table and thinking about the many differences between liberal and conservative values and attitudes, choose **one** of the following assignments to complete.

Create a 10-question survey to give to your classmates, family members, neighbors, or others. The survey should be designed to assess whether the respondent (the person taking the survey) is liberal or conservative, and to what degree (how convinced or serious is the person of his or her views?). The survey should also categorize people in any way that you think is meaningful (e.g., gender, age group, political party).

Give the survey to at least 15 people and report on the results. Your report should include the following headings and contents:

Title: Give your report a descriptive and interesting title.

Overview: Describe the number of people you surveyed and the categories of people you surveyed.

Results: Present your survey's results in a table that shows the percentages of responses to each question and degree. Also present a table that shows responses by category. You may combine your information and tables in the way that makes your results most clear.

Discussion: Write about your discoveries. What was particularly interesting? What was surprising? What would you ask next time? How would you improve the survey?

Appendix: Attach your survey as an appendix at the end of your report.

Create a method you can use to measure whether newspaper articles, news reports, online reports, columns, editorials, letters to the editor, speeches, essays, and other media presentations are conservative or liberal. (Social scientists sometimes call this method of research *content analysis*.) Besides determining whether the media pieces are either conservative or liberal, your method should also measure *to what degree* the media pieces are liberal or conservative. (Are they extreme in their views, or are their views barely detectable?) It is best to develop a measurement instrument that uses the methods you want to employ. The instrument should help you categorize the material you are considering and give it a rating (e.g., from 1–5) for how liberal or conservative it is.

Using your method and instrument, evaluate at least 10 media samples from different sources (e.g., TV interview, online opinion column, presidential speech, letter to the editor). Try to get a broad sample so that your research is not biased (i.e., 10 opinion columns from one author would be much too narrow a sample). Write a report summarizing your results and attach a copy of your research instrument. The report should contain the following headings and contents:

Title: Give your report an interesting and descriptive title.

Method: Include a copy of your method and instrument in your report, as well as a description. Describe how you chose the media samples that you studied.

Overview: Briefly describe your rationale for designing your instrument, and also describe the media pieces you chose to evaluate.

Results: Present your results in a narrative report, table, diagram, or whatever method works best. Be sure to remain neutral when presenting your information.

Discussion: What did you find out? Were more of the media pieces conservative or were more liberal? Did the source of the piece seem to matter? Did the subject of the piece make a difference? If you were to do this assignment again, how would you improve it? You can include your original opinions and ideas in this section.

Concept Sorting Key

Liberal	Conservative
Government control of industrial waste Regulations for landlords Federal law stating that all new cars will be energy-efficient	Tax breaks for energy-efficient cars Prayer in public schools Censorship of YouTube The Boy Scouts Industries monitoring their own waste Private charities for poor people instead of state programs

Name:_____ Date:_____

Political Science Rubric

	Excellent	Good	Needs work	Inadequate
Formatting and mechanics	Project is typed. Title and headings are present. Project contains very few errors.	Project is typed. Title and some headings are present. Project contains errors, but they are not distracting.	Project is typed and contains no headings, although it may have a title. Project has numerous distracting errors.	Project is handwritten or incomplete and contains many distracting errors that interfere with content.
Overview	Summary is brief but complete and gives a clear description of rationale, instrument, and so on.	Summary is brief but adequate and describes the necessary elements.	Summary is disorganized, unclear, or too brief.	Summary is missing information and is rambling or too brief.
Results	Materials clearly present all important information. Results are well organized and explained.	Materials are adequately organized and explained.	Materials are poorly organized, incomplete, or unclear.	Material is very disorganized, and information is missing, jumbled, or not explained.
Discussion	Discussion is insightful. Student makes thoughtful connections among concepts and data.	Discussion is complete and accurate. Student pairs data and concepts.	Discussion is poorly organized and lacks insight. Student simply lists or describes data without making connections.	Discussion is incomplete or disorganized. Student presents little or no data, or lists ideas or concepts and does not discuss them.
Appendix or instrument	Student included a clean copy in an appropriate spot. Survey or instrument was well designed to gather meaningful data.	Student included a clean copy in an appropriate spot. Survey or instrument was solid but could have been more in depth or relevant.	Student included a copy that was either messy or not well planned. Connections between concepts and survey or instrument may be unclear.	Student did not include a copy, or it was messy. Instrument was not well designed for tasks or concepts.

Total points: _____
Comments:

_____

_____

CHAPTER 10

Free Markets vs. Regulated Markets

Objectives

⚙ Students will analyze the merits and faults of a free market system.

⚙ Students will analyze the merits and faults of a regulated market.

⚙ Students will evaluate the vulnerabilities of consumers and producers in both free and regulated markets.

Introduction

A more radical (and perhaps more eye-catching) title for this chapter would have been "Communism vs. Capitalism." That title would have been inaccurate, however, because the broader debate is based on competing views about the market and its role in society.

In the 2010 edition of *The Encyclopedia Britannica*, the market is defined as "a means by which the exchange of goods and services takes place as a result of buyers and sellers being in contact with one another, either directly or through mediating agents or institutions." Early markets were indeed physical places. However, the more general modern definition illustrates that buyers and sellers no longer have to be in the same location at the same time. The advent of money and ongoing technological innovations have made the market a virtual entity, as opposed to a literal one.

In 1776, Adam Smith first proposed the concept of the market as a self-regulating system of exchange that enabled goods and services to be distributed from their source to consumers who needed them. Smith described the autonomous nature of the market: Consumers and producers, acting in their own best interests, would create a system whose design would be far superior to anything a government could engineer (Brown, 1995).

Smith regarded the market as having a vital function—it was a means to a social end. Smith's market made the distribution of products within an increasingly industrial urban (and colonial) society possible (Brown, 1995). For Smith, the market had almost miraculous powers to correct its own inevitable imbalances and adjust itself without intervention.

Smith's essential characterization of the market remains vital and alive in the popular imagination today. Although economists of every stripe continue to refine conceptions of the market, and to recognize weaknesses in the model, many people still idealize a self-regulating market as the optimum form of economic organization.

The core idea behind the free market concept was that economies could not be designed—they had to develop spontaneously around market exchanges. Policy should protect the market, not fiddle with it. Free market enthusiasts endorsed the concept of *laissez faire*, meaning "let [people] do they choose" in French. Supporters believed that society benefited from the initiative of individuals who were allowed to pursue their best interests in the market. To them, meddling with this pursuit was unacceptable. Interference with the market would induce chaos and collapse by divorcing people and companies from the genuine fruit of their efforts—profits.

Sowell (2006) pointed out that early free market economists were not so fierce in their beliefs as to approve unfair advantages for those with more capital than others. Smith himself favored the protection of laborers from what he viewed as an unfair and unbalanced market dominated by wealthy employers. Instead, his idea was that under optimum conditions, and with equal access to and distribution of capital, wealth would be spread around to those who participated in the market. To put it simply, the market would self-regulate in an equitable way.

Yogi Berra is reputed to have said, "In theory, there is no difference between theory and practice. In practice there is." He could easily have been talking about Adam Smith's free market. Unfortunately for Smith, the market did *not* equitably distribute wealth; it failed to self-regulate

(at least, without going through disastrous fluctuations), it was neither geographically nor temporally uniform, and it was never free from the manipulations of people with power, whether they were captains of industry or government officials.

Smith was writing during a time when the merchant class and craft guilds were shrugging off the bonds of feudal control that both Church and state had imposed until that point. This historic shift may have liberated many a cooper and shoemaker (at least, until barrel and shoe factories came into existence). However, as the industrial revolution expanded, economic forces conspired against both the average Europeans and the very poor ones (Schnitzer, 1991).

Karl Marx (1818–1883) identified the economic forces that were crushing laborers. If a person owned land or machines (e.g., a wool factory), then it was possible for that person to remain independent and make a profit. However, what if the only things a person had to sell were strength and time? In *The Communist Manifesto* (Marx & Engels, 1848), Marx identified the powerless laborers as the proletariat class, whose members "live only so long as they find work, and who find work only so long as their labor increases capital" (p. 41), and he went on to state that because laborers had only their bodies and time to offer to the market, they must literally sell themselves, becoming "like every other article of commerce" (p. 41). Furthermore, Marx explained that machinery, far from making labor easier, only added to the laborer's miserable plight, rendering the worker a mere extension of a machine. Marx proposed that the profits made by factory owners and others like them (the bourgeoisie) were in direct proportion to the time that laborers put into the products. He argued that besides the small amount of time per day that laborers spent on themselves, their labors only served to increase the value of the product, ultimately making the bourgeois owner even richer (Schnitzer, 1991). As more and more products were made, prices would go down, and the laborer would be no better off—and would perhaps be worse off.

Marx, his collaborator Engels, and the intellectuals and revolutionaries who followed them called for nothing short of a complete transformation of the market. They hoped that this revolution, led by the proletariat class, would culminate in workers seizing the means of production (capital) and establishing a transitional socialist state (Schnitzer, 1991). After they made dramatic reforms, private property would be abolished and society would spontaneously blossom into a communist association "in which the free development of each [was] the condition for the free development of all" (Marx & Engels, 1848, p. 53).

Quite obviously, this communist vision of the market represented ideas that were in complete opposition to Smith's ideas. Rather than leaving the market alone and trusting that it would nurture a system that could benefit all, Marx and his followers advocated for a political revolution in which the market would be seized in order to dull its sharp edges, eventually transforming a free market into an utterly tamed one. Interestingly enough, some of the social reforms mentioned in *The Communist Manifesto* were labor unions, graduated income tax, universal public education, child labor laws, and full political participation for women (Marx & Engels, 1848). All of these ideas, radical in Marx's day, have become normative under legislative reforms within capitalist countries.

Analyzing the success or failure of communist states is beyond the scope of this book. It is sufficient to state that communism—at least as envisioned by Marxists—appears to have failed. Marxist economies have seemed to freeze in place after their governments took over production. In this way, communism—meant to liberate workers—ended up exploiting them while profiting at an international level.

As with most of the oppositions discussed in this book, it is nearly impossible to find a concrete example of a pure version of either concept. North Korea certainly has a tightly regulated market, which has led to a serious decrease in the quality of life for its citizens. Likewise, unfettered markets were prevalent in the early days of the industrial revolution, a time when workers were often exploited. Today, some markets (e.g., in France) have many controls, whereas others (e.g., in the United States) have relatively few restrictions.

The question may not be whether we should completely regulate the market or embrace a full laissez faire system. Instead, people must determine how much regulation is necessary. Perhaps it is our task to strike a delicate balance between the stimulating profit motives of a free market and the necessary protections offered by regulation, including product safety standards, minimum wage statutes, and pollution guidelines.

Classroom Activities and Assessment

The Talk Show Battle (pp. 160–161) is an activity that has students research the pros and cons of a garment industry in the fictional developing country of Denimstan as they prepare for a debate on *NewsNow*, a local news program. **Case Study: The Performance Rights Act** (pp. 162–164) is a brief article on regulation in the music industry. The article is followed by questions to help students understand how regulating a market can cause controversy. **Propaganda** (p. 165) is a poster-making assignment in which students are assigned roles and then create propaganda posters either for or against a free market approach to a given issue. You can divide the students into groups and assign the roles and topics, or students can select the topics that they address with their posters. There are many interesting potential options, including environmental regulations, free trade agreements, ethanol production, taxes on tobacco, lawsuits against monopolies, reforms in China, minimum wage laws, and public access to television and radio. This is an advanced assignment that will require some structuring by the teacher and student research skills. In addition to the materials provided, you may wish to have your students read portions of *The Communist Manifesto*, parts of which are surprisingly accessible to students. A general overview of **evaluation criteria** is provided at the end of the chapter (p. 166), but it is up to you how to have students complete these activities, as well as how they are evaluated.

The Talk Show Battle

This assignment requires students to create an informed debate that will occur on air during *NewsNow*, a local news show. Students may write scripts and perform them live, or they may videotape their performance. They may also wish to conduct the debate spontaneously, without a script, so that it is more in the style of an actual on-air debate.

Assign this exercise to groups of 3–5 students. One student will play the role of host and moderator on *NewsNow*. The other 2–4 students will be guests on the show and will play the following roles (multiple students can play these roles, depending on the size of the group):

- CEO of Mean-Jeans, the top designer label of jeans and other apparel sold throughout the United States, Japan, the United Kingdom, Australia, and Canada

- Founder of Consumer Watchdogs, a nonprofit organization that monitors the working conditions and product quality of the apparel industry

---

Background

According to Consumer Watchdogs, Mean-Jeans has several manufacturing facilities in the country of Denimstan. This country is very poor, with high rates of unemployment. Denimstan does not have labor unions, worker insurance, or minimum wage laws. Regulations regarding pollution and job safety are rarely enforced. The average wage in the country is approximately $5.00 per day (in American dollars). Mean-Jeans pays its Denimstan workers the equivalent of $7.00 per day.

Consumer Watchdogs wants Mean-Jeans to pay its workers better and accuses Mean-Jeans of making huge profits by paying its Denimstan workers so little, offering no insurance, and caring little about worker safety regulations.

The CEO of Mean-Jeans refuses to cooperate with Consumer Watchdogs and points out that Mean-Jeans pays its factory workers more than they could make almost anywhere else in Denimstan. The CEO also says that Mean-Jeans are popular because they are inexpensive, and paying workers more would simply cause the price to go up, resulting in fewer sales and making the company go bankrupt—and then all of the workers would lose their jobs.

Students may choose their character names and as much scripting and costuming as you direct or allow. Students will need to do some

research on the disparities (in economy and in quality of life) between industrialized nations and the developing world. They will also need to explore how the garment industry operates (e.g., wholesale prices, retail markup) and how corporations operate. (If your class schedule permits you to spend a few extra days on this activity, you might choose to make it an interdisciplinary project.)

Students supporting Mean-Jeans will need to gather some data on American consumers and their spending habits. They could also research how American companies have affected workers and working conditions in other counties. They should explore whether American shoppers are willing to spend more and buy domestic products, and how this impacts foreign workers.

Case Study: The Performance Rights Act

In 2009, members of both the House of Representatives and the Senate proposed a bill called the Performance Rights Act and recommended that Congress pass the bill. Legislators supporting this bill stated that it would close a legal loophole that had existed for almost a century. The loophole, part of the Copyright Act, allowed AM and FM radio stations to be exempt from having to pay record companies for airing music played by their artists. This meant that if the bill became a law, radio stations would need to pay a fee (called a royalty fee) to recording companies for playing songs the companies owned.

Satellite, cable, and streaming Internet radio stations already had to pay royalty fees to recording companies, but traditional radio stations did not. Naturally, these alternative radio stations (satellite, cable, Internet) wanted the traditional radio stations to have to follow the same rules that they did. They claimed that it was unfair competition and that Congress should level the playing field.

Hundreds of recording artists agreed and thought that all radio stations should have to pay, including Jay-Z, Jewel, Bruce Springsteen, Ludacris, and the estate of Tupac Shakur. If traditional radio stations had to pay record companies to use artists' music, then those artists stood to earn more in royalties for their songs—their royalties came from actual music sales, as opposed to whether or not their songs were simply played.

Radio stations argued that the new law would effectively be a tax on their business. They argued that recording artists benefited from the airtime they received and from being featured on the radio; the traditional radio stations viewed this as free advertising. Furthermore, they claimed that about half of any money generated from the proposed fees would go to the recording companies, rather than to the artists. They also claimed that most of this money would go overseas to foreign record labels.

But small radio stations—such as student-run college stations and urban stations owned by minority entrepreneurs—complained about the new bill. These stations said that they would go out of business if they had to pay fees for the music that they played. Congress responded by saying that smaller stations would pay less than bigger ones.

Radio stations also claimed that new artists would suffer from this law, arguing that no radio station would want to gamble on playing a new artist's music if the station had to pay the same fee they would pay for music from a well-recognized artist.

Things in the music industry got ugly. Several artists said that after they had publicly declared support for the Performance Rights act, they were singled out and boycotted by radio stations. (At least one station in Texas openly admits to having done this.) The Federal Communications Commission became involved.

In the days before the Internet, downloads, and streaming, the music market was simpler. People liked what they heard on the radio or at a friend's house, and they went to stores and bought physical copies for themselves. Now, though, it is rare to find a store selling only CDs. Presently, a large percentage of music is sold from a digital platform like iTunes. Frighteningly, the International Federation of the Phonographic Industry (IFPI) reported that in 2009, approximately 95% of all music downloads were illegal—swiped for free from the Internet. Such statistics make it clear that the rules surrounding the music market have changed forever. The conflict over the Performance Rights Act inspires a few important questions; the answers to these questions will impact the future of the music industry.

Sources

IFPI.org. (2009). *IFPI publishes digital music report 2009*. Retrieved from http://www.ifpi.org/content/section_resources/dmr2009.html

Lasar, M. (2009). *Is radio suppressing pro performance rights act artists?* Retrieved from http://arstechnica.com/media/news/2009/08/is-radio-suppressing-pro-performance-rights-act-artists.ars

MusicFirst Coalition. (2010). Retrieved from http://musicfirstcoalition.org

Williams, G. (2009 July 27). Growing opposition to the Performance Rights Act [Web log post]. Retrieved from http://radio2020.wordpress.com/2009/07/27/growing-opposition-to-the-performance-rights-act

Questions

1. Do radio stations offer free advertising for musicians? What do radio stations sell?

2. Could you argue that it is fair for streaming or satellite radio stations to pay record labels for the music they play, while traditional radio stations don't have to pay?

3. Small stations and public radio stations offer services to the community. They must make free public service announcements and

host local talk shows to get information out to citizens. Should they be protected for this reason?

4. Should the government leave the radio market alone, or have radio stations operated outside of a fair market for too long?

5. Is the Performance Rights Act an example of taxing and meddling with the music and radio market? Why or why not?

Propaganda

Group 1

Role: Pro-Market Propaganda Writer (alternate titles include Spin Doctor, Publicist, Speechwriter, Promoter, and Image Consultant)

Audience: General public

Format: Propaganda poster (with list of sources on the back)

Topic: The importance of a free market. Your poster should point out the benefits of having a free market or the negative consequences of limiting or controlling the market (you will need to research this). You can make the poster about the market in general or about a specific market (e.g., healthcare).

Group 2

Role: Anti-Market Propaganda Writer (alternate titles include Leftist, Pundit, Radical, and Agitator)

Audience: General public

Format: Propaganda poster (with list of sources on the back)

Topic: The importance of controlling the market. Your poster should point out the benefits of controlling the market or the negative consequences of allowing a free market (you will need to research this). You can make the poster about controlling the market in general or about a specific market (e.g., prescription drugs).

Poster Expectations

Design: Your poster should be colorful, eye-catching, neat, and well made, and its illustrations should be consistent with your topic or theme.

Text: Your poster should have a title, a slogan, and one paragraph explaining your topic. Use strong words, but do not make your claims ridiculous. Your poster should include no spelling, usage, capitalization, or punctuation errors.

Topic: The information you present should be persuasive, but not exaggerated or inappropriate.

Evaluation Criteria

Talk Show Battle

- ☼ The final product should demonstrate that the student is familiar with terms, practices, and related current events (e.g., the GDP, minimum wage, literacy rates, workers' benefits, wholesale prices, history).

- ☼ The student should demonstrate appropriate conduct, befitting of a public forum debate or interview.

- ☼ The student should have an organized method or argument.

- ☼ The student should summarize the main point of view and reasoning.

Case Study: The Performance Rights Act

If you assign the questions as an assignment or as journal entries, then students should answer them in complete sentences, demonstrate logic and insight, and justify their reasoning with evidence from the article (or from further reading or knowledge).

Propaganda

- ☼ The poster should demonstrate an appropriate example and understanding of the student's assigned position (either favoring a free market or favoring market regulations).

- ☼ The poster should demonstrate evidence of research in its content and should include a list of sources.

- ☼ The poster should use color, be neat, include illustrations and a title, and demonstrate thoughtfulness regarding design.

- ☼ The poster's text should use persuasive language and correct spelling, usage, grammar, and punctuation.

11

Safety vs. Risk

Objectives

○ Students will evaluate and describe how the tension between safety and risk influences our actions and decisions.

○ Students will identify and evaluate the tension between safety and risk in literature, especially as it drives characters' actions and plot.

○ After learning about the essential features of the Dionysian and Apollonian temperaments, students will be able to identify them as demonstrated by characters in literature.

○ Students will analyze the concepts of delayed vs. immediate gratification.

Introduction

According to Greek myth, Daedalus was a clever architect and engineer who fell into disfavor with his employer. As a result, he and his teenaged son, Icarus, were imprisoned in an outdoor maze that he had designed. Daedalus's work on this maze was so brilliant that not even he, its creator, could escape it. Being an optimist, however, he did not despair. Instead, he fashioned two sets of wings out of feathers and wax. Together, Daedalus and Icarus soared away from their prison.

The older and less impetuous Daedalus warned Icarus to steer a middle course between the sun and the ocean below. But Icarus was so enamored of his new gift of flight that he did not heed his father's advice and impulsively flew too close to the sun. Tragically, his wings melted and he fell to his death, disappearing under the waves forever (Hamilton, 1942).

The story of Icarus and Daedalus is ancient, but the conundrum of balancing the requirement for safety with the equally important need to take risks extends back to the dawn of time: Ever since the first unicellular creatures ventured forth in the primordial seas and attempted to eat without being eaten, living creatures have had to weigh the rewards of risk against the necessary amounts of safety. Although it is unlikely that simple creatures have enough self-awareness to worry about dangers in their environment, it is clear that increasing brainpower enables more advanced species—human beings, for instance—to more accurately assess (and imagine) danger signals.

The necessity of balancing safety and risk shows up in daily decisions, financial planning, and speculative musings about fate. The interplay between safety and risk does not just animate our lives—it is also what stratifies markets and infuses the arts with a compelling tension.

Like many young people, Icarus failed to listen to his father's warnings. Parenting requires a great deal of vigilance as mothers and fathers watch over and warn children about risks in their environment. How closely parents supervise their children may vary, but watching over children is hardwired into parents' brains, and children have a corresponding attachment to their parents.

Researchers have demonstrated that planning (such as Daedalus's plan to avoid flying too close to the sun) is mediated in the prefrontal cortex (Carter & Frith, 2000). This is the outer layer of the brain located in the forehead region. Brain cells in the prefrontal cortex do not begin developing into a mature state until adolescence. As a result, parents function as a child's prefrontal cortex until he or she grows one.

Curiously, the neurons in an adolescent's prefrontal cortex undergo explosive growth in the early teen years, and then they progressively die off in a process called *pruning* (Bainbridge, 2009). The process of pruning is not harmful; instead, it allows the prefrontal lobe to develop efficient pathways for important tasks and functions. Useful paths become highways, while less useful ones disappear.

Pruning in the adolescent's prefrontal cortex is accompanied by equally dramatic changes in the brain's interior. One of these changes enables dopamine, a powerful neurochemical that determines levels of arousal and motivation, to be linked and routed between structures of the brain that govern pleasure-seeking and the operations of the prefrontal cortex (Bainbridge, 2009). If all goes well, then by the end of adolescence, a person has a brain that is uniquely programmed to guide that person towards desired ends (such as food) while also planning to avoid unnecessary risks.

The transition period between early adolescence and adulthood, when the prefrontal cortex is not fully developed, may be fraught with danger. Until this development is complete, many adolescents are prone to engaging in risky behavior. Some theorists propose that teen risk taking is simply a consequence of the fact that the prefrontal cortex is less developed, leading to impaired impulse control. Another interesting hypothesis is that during adolescent development, structural changes in the brain make it less sensitive to neurotransmitters that create the sense of pleasure. As a result, some teenagers need to engage in more extreme behavior to get the same thrill that others would get from less extreme activities (Bainbridge, 2009). These teens may find themselves doing wheelies on icy roads instead of playing ping-pong. Regardless of whether an underdeveloped prefrontal cortex, neurotransmitter irregularities, or other factors are to blame, the bottom line is the same: As car insurance bills attest, teens are much more likely than adults are to engage in risky behavior.

Watching YouTube videos of adults engaging in foolish activities will demonstrate that some people don't seem to grow out of the type of risk-taking behavior characterized by an immature prefrontal lobe. Whether they are freefalling from the edge of a cliff in a bat suit, riding bulls, or driving a stock car, some risk takers actively seek out activities most of us would avoid. Scientific investigations have shown that these people are unique; neuroscientists have labeled them *novelty seekers*. Researchers have even isolated a gene sequence—the dopamine receptor gene D4— that appears to be responsible for novelty seeking (Tasler, 2008). In most individuals, this gene sequence repeats itself four times, but in the novelty-seeking population, it repeats seven times. This sequence repetition makes those people who carry it less susceptible to the usual rewarding effects of dopamine. As a result, like teenagers who drive too fast, they must take bolder risks to generate the same level of arousal that typical people get from novel experiences (Tasler, 2008).

Not surprisingly, this population was discovered during research on Attention Deficit/Hyperactivity Disorder (ADHD). A little more than half of the population with ADHD displays the novelty-seeking genetic sequence. Oddly, they don't appear to have many of the cognitive problems associated with this mysterious condition. Their supposed deficits in attention have more to do with a need for speed and action, not an inability to concentrate (Tasler, 2008).

So if risk-taking behavior is inevitable (at least for a period of time) for teenagers as their brains develop and inevitable for others (permanently) who are genetically hardwired to seek adventure, then why haven't these people been weeded out by evolution? After all, we might assume that novelty-seeking behavior such as skydiving or fishtailing a sports car would result in a shorter life and not many offspring.

Safety is clearly a crucial factor for survival, and there is a good reason why the overwhelming majority of human beings instinctively seek safety. However, risk is also necessary. A species cannot survive and evolve without risk. Animals must venture forth and seek food, shelter, mates, and promising habitats. All of these rewarding outcomes are achieved only at the price of some risk.

Modern human beings are rarely exposed to the sorts of risks that our ancestors were, but we are still aware of the need to balance risk with reward. We know that without taking a risk, we may not be able to exploit an opportunity and enjoy its rewards. Stock investors recognize this, along with venture capitalists, entrepreneurs, inventors, political leaders, and others who stir things up to see what opportunities may arise. Greater risks often lead to bigger payoffs—this wasn't the case with Icarus, but it was with the Wright brothers.

The advantages of risk taking, then, have perpetuated novelty-seeking behavior in our species. Those who gambled and won undoubtedly attracted mates and transferred their risk-taking legacies to the next generation.

So it is clear that risk can benefit human beings, both individually and as a species. But what about safety? There are real dangers in the world—everything from dangers our ancestors feared, such as tigers, to modern dangers, such as guns. In monkey societies, females outnumber males largely because males are more likely to take impulsive risks and die from their reckless decisions. Greg Vicino, head primatologist at the San Diego Zoo, remarked that in dangerous settings, "the impulsive monkeys get smoked" (Tasler, 2008, p. 51). Unless we are very lucky, virtually all of us are here because we have made wise enough choices to survive—driving on the highway, swimming in the ocean, and participating in other risky situations. Most of us can recall situations where

we did not make wise decisions, and usually, such memories are accompanied by a sigh of relief that things did not go wrong for us.

Playing it safe usually pays off. In the stock market and with horse races, playing it safe usually offers people modest rewards that sustain them, and these people will never know whether bolder choices would have led to greater advantages. Often, people who play it safe comfort themselves by recalling the misfortune of others who took more risks, and they dismiss stories about big gamblers who won, saying that these people just got really lucky (which is usually the case).

There is a reason why we are attracted to the warm glow coming from cottage windows on winter nights, and why we rest a little easier once we've paid our bills. We crave safety. The stress of prolonged exposure to danger—whether from a natural disaster or from the threat of bankruptcy—causes human beings to suffer physical and psychological consequences. Safety is more than a need; it is a right. According to Article 3 of *The Universal Declaration of Human Rights* (United Nations, 1948), "Everyone has the right to life, liberty and security of person."

Indeed, it is important to remember the countless people around the world—both civilians and soldiers—who struggle to remain alive while trapped in war zones. Others face immense risk every day as they try to make a living in barren fields or streets strewn with garbage. Is it ethical for the adrenaline junkies among us to risk their lives for amusement while so many others are desperately trying to preserve their own lives? Isn't this a bit like grilling a delicious steak next door to a soup kitchen and then tossing it in the garbage?

Nobody is attracted to obvious risks that offer no conceivable rewards. We are tempted by risks that promise something in return, such as enviable fame, status, thrills, pleasure, or profits. Most decisions, whether they are trivial or critical, require us to assess the balance between safety and risk. When we do this, we must also take our own temperament into account.

Financial advisors will remind you about your "tolerance for risk" when choosing a suite of investments for your retirement account. Most of us compromise by choosing something in between the extremes of risk (volatile stocks) and safety (steady treasury bonds), and most people take fewer risks as they get older.

Career decisions require us to balance largely unattainable desires with less desirable (but more attainable) goals. One influential theory (Gottfredson, 2002) regarding career choice focuses on the processes of *circumscription* and *compromise* (pp. 92–93). Young people engage in circumscription when they progressively rule out unacceptable types of work to arrive at a more realistic menu of acceptable careers. They engage in compromise when they abandon their strongest preferences in favor of less desirable careers that they know are more accessible. Career decisions require both circumscription and compromise, although too much of either may lead to a lifetime of frustration.

Young people are still in the process of circumscription (Gottfredson, 2002). They are ruling out career choices that may not fit. Some unfortunate youths may be forced by financial situations (or other factors) to compromise rather quickly. The process of selecting a career has not always been a part of culture or human history (e.g., during slavery or serfdom, for women, or in tribes). In spite of these factors, the dynamic opposition of risk and safety plays itself out as we choose our life's work.

Novels exploit the rich material generated as characters take risks and seek safety. During the rising action of a plot, the protagonist is often forced to sacrifice safety in order to solve a certain problem or achieve a certain goal. By the time the plot reaches its climactic point, safety is no longer assured, and the protagonist is taking major risks. Other storylines explore regrets and ill consequences of past decisions. Characters may grapple with the frustrations of having settled for too little or the harsh realities of having risked too much.

The German philosopher Friedrich Nietszche, in *The Birth of Tragedy* (1886/1967) first explored Greek literature by examining the dynamic tension between two general temperaments he called *Apollonian* and *Dionysian*. These temperaments were named after the Greek gods Apollo and Dionysius, respectively, and have become commonplace in scholarly writing.

The Apollonian temperament is characterized by self-control, order, structure, reason, logic, restraint, and safety. Science and logic are largely Apollonian pursuits. In contrast, the Dionysian temperament is characterized by passion, spontaneity, impulsivity, emotion, romanticism, and risk. Many aspects of art, drama, and music are Dionysian. Actually, though, every person—from the most logical of scientists to the most spontaneous of artists—must still incorporate both the Apollonian and Dionysian approaches into life. We need both structure and spontaneity in order to accomplish anything and remain sane. All people, however, differ in where they may find themselves on the continuum between the Dionysian and Apollonian temperaments. Sometimes they will break the usual pattern: For instance, a middle-aged banker may suddenly drop out of society and become a musician and artist. Likewise, a young rock musician may decide to become a marketer and music producer. These dynamic tensions continue to animate lives, both real and fictional.

Classroom Activities and Assessments

Playing It Safe or Going for Broke (pp. 174–177) is a short script depicting a conversation between college students. The dialogue—which explores safety, risk, decisions, and hypocrisy—may be read silently or aloud in class to inspire either journaling or discussion. **Shopping With Friends and Plastic** (pp. 178–179; questions on pp. 180–181) is an expository essay on the dangers of mixing immediate gratification and credit cards; it lends itself well to discussion, summary writing, and journaling. **Paddling With the Toga Boys** (pp. 182–185) is a short story that dramatizes the contrasting traits of the Dionysian and Apollonian temperaments; following the story are questions that may be used as journal or discussion prompts. **Apollonian vs. Dionysian Character Study** (pp. 186–187) is an assignment requiring students to analyze the protagonist in a book they have read (or a film they have seen) and to classify that character on a spectrum ranging from Dionysian to Apollonian. Then, students analyze how that character's risk taking affects his or her decisions. **Dissecting a Decision** (p. 188) is an exercise that asks students to assess an important decision they have made to determine how they evaluated the safety and risk associated with a given situation. A general overview of **evaluation criteria** is provided at the end of the chapter (p. 189), but it is up to you how to have students complete these activities, as well as how they are evaluated.

Playing It Safe or Going for Broke

> **Characters:** Josh and Quentin, high school seniors; Josh's older sister Laney, a college student; and Laney's former roommate Aliyah, who recently graduated from college
>
> **Scene:** Late evening in early spring; Josh and Quentin are on an orientation visit to Creston College, Laney's school. They are relaxing in Laney's apartment, which is littered with books, laundry, dirty cereal bowls, and gear from a recent camping trip. Aliyah is visiting campus for a job fair.

Aliyah: *(pointing at a few dirty socks scattered on the coffee table)* I see that your interior decorating skills haven't changed, Laney.

Laney: I'll clean my laundry when it can crawl to the washing machine by itself.

Aliyah: Yech! So, Josh, are either you or Quentin going to be speaking at your graduation?

Josh: Nope.

Quentin: I know the guy who's speaking.

Laney: Who is it—Miller?

Quentin: How'd you guess?

Laney: That whole family is full of geniuses. His sister got a full-ride scholarship to Yale.

Josh: And the keynote speaker is going to be the mayor.

Aliyah: It doesn't matter who gives the speech—they all sound pretty much the same!

Quentin: What do you mean?

Aliyah: Here, I'll give you my outline. It fits 97% of all graduation speeches. It goes like this: First, the speaker says, "Four years ago, you probably didn't think this day would ever come." Next comes something about how anything is possible for this graduating class as long as the students try. Then the speaker tells everyone to work hard to ensure that they achieve their dreams, dreams made possible by the solid academic foundation provided by good old whatever high school!

Laney: A little bitter, are we? What would you prefer them to say?

Aliyah: The truth would be very refreshing. You have to make a living, you can't just have fun all of the time, and most of your dreams aren't possible, no matter how hard you work. A person may want to be an artist, but with an art degree, he'll probably end up washing dishes for a living. You have to compromise your dreams, not chase after them.

Josh: But you don't want to discourage people. It's graduation—speakers need to be inspirational.

Aliyah: I know. I don't think it's right to just depress people for no reason, but those graduation speeches are totally hypocritical. You've got to be realistic and tell people how it really is.

Quentin: But people might give up too early. Maybe some of us will achieve our dream careers.

Josh: Yeah, you never know.

Laney: Yeah, Aliyah, you jaded oldster!

Aliyah: Hey, I'm not bitter, OK? But look at the damage you do when you tell people that they can achieve some dream that is actually impossible. That does more harm than being straight with them. I knew a guy who changed his major from music to accounting because he realized he'd have loans to pay off. He finally grew up and realized that his little garage band probably wasn't going to make it big.

Quentin: What if everybody did that?

Aliyah: More people would be employed.

Quentin: But we wouldn't have many great artists or actors. Nobody would have taken a risk and tried.

Aliyah: We have too many artists and actors as it is.

Laney: I'm a drama major, and I'm not afraid.

Aliyah: You should be.

Laney: But Aliyah, you majored in literature!

Aliyah: I did, and now I'm working in a bank. I should have taken more business courses—I would be getting paid better now if I had.

Josh: Didn't you like literature courses, though?

Aliyah: Sure, I loved them. But look where it got me.

Quentin: Don't you like your job?

Aliyah: It's OK. I wanted to be a novelist or a journalist. Then I saw what a beginning journalist makes per paycheck, and I realized I wouldn't be able to pay off my loans and have a place of my own.

Quentin: So you compromised, played it safe.

Aliyah: I played it the only way I could.

Laney: I'm going for broke. I'll take a risk and move to L.A.

Aliyah: When you say going for broke, you probably don't realize you might really *be* broke! Don't risk it all and bus tables all so you can be an extra on a movie set.

Josh: I kind of see what you mean about people being hypocrites!

Laney: *(joking)* Look, you've poisoned my little brother!

Aliyah: *(smiling)* Who are you talking about, Josh? Who are the hypocrites?

Josh: I don't know, just *(making quotation mark gestures)* "them" in general. You know, the people we all listen to. It's like all of the voices of parents, teachers, coaches, and ministers—all of them just blend into one voice.

Quentin: Whoa Josh, you're getting a little delusional here.

Josh: No, I just mean that they all say a lot of the same things. They tell you to work hard, but then they tell you to relax and not to get stressed. They tell you not to get too serious with your girlfriend, but then they take millions of pictures before prom. They tell you one thing and then expect you to do another. So why shouldn't they tell us to dream big, and then tell us to grow up and get practical?

Quentin: My sister was saying something sort of similar yesterday. She said that some teen magazine she reads had a big article about eating disorders, but they had a very skinny model on the cover, and last month, they had an article about how obese teens were getting. She said they were sending girls mixed messages—extreme ones that didn't give them a healthy view of reality.

Josh: Yeah, that's what I'm talking about. They don't ever tell it to you straight.

Laney: Maybe you just have to decide for yourself.

Aliyah: *(with heavy irony)* That's a surprisingly good point, Laney!

Laney: I was always brilliant—you just took it for granted when you were my roommate.

Quentin: But what if *(gesturing quotation marks)* "they" don't really know the answers to our questions? Maybe they're just as confused as we are.

Laney: About what?

Quentin: You know, about decisions like what to do with your life, or who to marry, or whether you should follow your dreams or not. You can take a risk and then regret it, but you can regret *not* taking a risk, too—like if you play it too safe and don't give the garage band a try.

Josh: So it's all about them looking back and not wanting us to take too many risks?

Quentin: No, I'm sure they are worried about both—taking too many risks, but also letting dreams get away.

Aliyah: Then how come they always sound like they know what we're supposed to do?

Quentin: Beats me—but I'm not sure I'm going to listen to anybody.

Aliyah: Hang on—they probably know a little more than we do. I'd rather listen to somebody who has lived through difficult situations before, who has some experience.

Quentin: Why? They could be wrong, too. Maybe they played it too safe.

Questions

1. Do you agree with Aliyah's assessment of graduation speeches? Why or why not?

2. Would it be better if graduation speakers "just told the truth"?

3. Are Laney and Quentin right? Is it wise to ignore advice and take more risks with your career plans?

4. Is Josh right? Do "they" all sound alike?

5. Do you think you will have to compromise between your dream career and a career in which you could make more money?

6. If you were to participate in this conversation, with whom would you agree?

7. If you spoke to Aliyah, what would you tell her?

8. If you spoke to Laney or Quentin, what would you say?

Shopping With Friends and Plastic

Oscar Wilde once said, "I can resist anything but temptation." His ironic statement could apply to any of us: According to an article in *Science Daily*, an online publication that summarizes important research, nearly all people tend to overestimate their ability to resist temptation. Furthermore, studies suggest that people who report the greatest confidence in their ability to exercise self-control are actually the least capable of doing so ("Temptation More Powerful," 2009)!

For many years, behavioral psychologists have referred to self-control as the capacity to *delay gratification*. The longer that you can put off getting something desirable and rewarding, like a nice slice of cheesecake, the better you are at delaying gratification. Likewise, the little devil on your shoulder is telling you to seek *immediate gratification* by suggesting that you go ahead and have the cheesecake right away.

There are a couple of powerful factors that play into whether you yield to immediate gratification. First, being around others who are poor at delaying gratification will lead you astray. This is not just something one of your parents would say; researchers have discovered that even *thinking* about a friend who has poor self-control causes people to perform more poorly than usual on tests that measure delayed gratification ("Self-Control," 2010).

> [R]esearchers have discovered that even *thinking* about a friend who has poor self-control causes people to perform more poorly than usual on tests that measure delayed gratification . . .

Second, any environmental feature that reduces a person's ability to resist impulses will impair that person's ability to delay gratification. This is why casinos serve alcohol to gamblers; once they have had a few drinks, they cannot resist gambling, even if they have already told themselves they have spent too much money. This is also why companies spend so much money on advertising, packaging, and displaying products. Everything is consciously designed to erode your resistance and to entice you.

With this information in mind, let's examine a common scenario. Let's imagine that you are at the mall with a few friends, and a couple of them are big spenders who love to shop. Furthermore, let's assume that you have a credit card. The situation just described is poisonous. First, the presence of an impulsive friend or two would be enough to influence you to make the same type of decisions that they do—namely, if you see them giving in to temptation and buying items (even items they do not need), you are much likelier to act similarly. Second, credit cards make it very easy to purchase products without facing any immediate consequences. Checkbooks are similar. At least when you see money leaving your wallet or purse, you have a visual cue reminding you about what you are spending. With credit cards, the cash disappearing with every transaction is invisible.

There is another way that credit cards make it too easy for people to spend money. The companies that own the cards offer to lend you money if you cannot pay their monthly bills. The problem with this is that credit card companies will charge three times as much interest as a bank would. Of course, some people cannot get a loan from a bank, so they are stuck borrowing money on their credit cards. Once people get caught in this trap, it is very difficult for them to dig themselves out.

Young people need to be especially careful with credit cards. Card companies will tell you that owning a credit card is a good thing—that it will help you build up a good credit rating (a score that lets lenders know how well you can handle your debts). They are right that it is important to build up your credit rating. However, a person needs to be very, very careful in order to built up credit without going into debt or ruining his or her credit. According to College Student Credit Card (2008), on any given month, only about 55% percent of college students pay off their credit card debts. If you choose to get a card someday, the best thing you can do is use it to make small purchases you can easily pay off, such as a pair of jeans. This is enough to show that you can pay for what you owe, which will establish a good credit rating for you. Never use the card as a source for borrowing money!

Counselors often tell students to trust themselves, and they encourage you to have good self-esteem. However, credit card companies and retailers don't care about your self-esteem—and in this case, neither should you. As the previously cited research showed, when it comes to self-control, people should not trust themselves. Too many people spend money they do not have, telling themselves that they deserve rewards and promising themselves to make up for it later on.

If you have a credit card, use it only for some small, scheduled purchases. Take cash with you instead when you go shopping; that way, you can see what you have spend and what you have left. Finally, if a friend of yours is an impulse buyer, spend time with him or her in other ways besides shopping. You do deserve to have fun, but something isn't fun if it comes back to bite you later on!

Shopping With Friends and Plastic

Questions

Answer the following questions, using extra paper as needed.

1. What features of this article make it an example of persuasive writing? Is it persuasive to you?

   _____

   _____

   _____

   _____

2. Summarize the article in one or two paragraphs. List two quotes from the article that you thought weren't important enough to put in your summary. Why did you leave these out?

   _____

   _____

   _____

   _____

   _____

   _____

   _____

   _____

   _____

3. Will you follow the author's advice? Why or why not?

   _____

   _____

   _____

   _____

4. Do you plan on having a credit card by the time you go to college? Do you want one sooner? Why or why not?

_____

_____

_____

_____

_____

5. When (or if) you get a credit card, how might you avoid overspending with it?

_____

_____

_____

_____

_____

6. Why might the concept of *delayed gratification* be more accurate and useful than *self-control*?

_____

_____

_____

_____

_____

Paddling With the Toga Boys

It was a warm afternoon in June, and the river was perfect. The spring rains were over, and the water wasn't too high, but it was swift enough to easily carry us along. I caught the aroma of pine and birch trees on the bluffs above, and occasionally I saw an eagle soaring on the updrafts. As our canoe drifted around one bend in the river and past a logjam on the downstream side, I heard a familiar whisper that I knew would soon be a roar. *Rapids*! I could already feel the air getting cooler, and I saw mist floating above the large boulders at the entrance of . . . wait a minute. I grabbed the map. It was the Devil's Playground. This was a Class II rapid—maybe even a Class III, if the water was high. If the water *was* high enough to make it a Class III, then only experienced canoeists should attempt it, and then only with flotation bags or a spray cover.

I knew that it would be a good idea to park the canoe and carry it around the rapids, but how many times do you get a chance to run the Devil's Playground? Riding a bucking canoe down a chute of whitewater surrounded by hissing rocks is like drinking a whole mug of adrenaline—it's a mix of serene concentration and fear that can't be described in words. I really wanted to do it, but the possibility that higher water had turned the rapid into a Class III worried me.

I thought Jared was being pretty quiet in the back, especially because rapids usually scare the living daylights out of him. I turned back to talk with him and that's when I discovered that something very strange was going on. Sitting at the stern of the canoe was a young guy with curly hair. He seemed to be dressed in a bed sheet, and he had sunscreen on his nose. I looked a little closer at him and saw that he was wearing a toga! He was holding something that looked like a ukulele or a violin. I dropped my paddle into the water in sheer amazement.

> **Sitting at the stern of the canoe was a young guy with curly hair. He seemed to be dressed in a bed sheet, and he had sunscreen on his nose.**

"Here you go, my friend—you'll be in serious need of this paddle really soon!" said someone to my right. I looked over, and directly beside the canoe was another guy in a toga. He had rescued my paddle and was holding it out to me—and floating on a giant, yellow rubber ducky! This guy looked like he'd had a rough night and definitely needed a shave. He was sporting a pair of stylish sunglasses, and he grinned mischievously at me.

"Where's Jared?" I asked the Toga Boys, wondering if I was hallucinating.

"Don't worry, we'll bring him back soon," the one in the back of the canoe assured me.

"Who are you guys?" I demanded. "What's going on?"

"Relax," said the guy in my canoe. "I'm the one who wanted to talk to you," he told me, "but party boy"—he nodded at the fellow on the rubber ducky—"insisted on coming along."

"But . . . but . . . !" I stuttered. They could tell I was afraid, like a fish caught in a net.

The guy on the giant rubber ducky calmly told me, "Chill out. I'm Dionysus, and the total killjoy in the back of your canoe is Apollo." I looked towards Apollo and could see that it annoyed him to be called a killjoy.

"Look, Dion," said Apollo. "I didn't have to bring you—besides, you owe me big time for covering for you to Zeus last weekend."

"So I'm supposed to believe that you guys are Greek gods?" I said.

"Hey, this one's not *completely* out of it," Dionysus remarked to Apollo. "There may be some hope for mortals after all."

"It's possible, but you've been wrong before," replied Apollo. "Remember that mortal in Crete, the one I told you not to get involved with?"

"Princess Ariadne," Dionysus said, suddenly looking very depressed. "Did you have to remind me?"

"Oops," Apollo said. "I'm sorry—I didn't mean to bring down the mood."

"Yeah right, killjoy," snapped Dionysus.

"I'm not a killjoy!" retorted Apollo. "I happen to have some personal ethics, that's all."

I could see that their bickering was only going to get worse, and even if I was hallucinating, I had some quick thinking to do before I reached the Devil's Playground. "Could you guys stop arguing?" I begged. "We're drifting towards the rapids!"

"That's right!" yelled Dionysus. "Woohoo!" He started rocking the rubber ducky back and forth and making quacking noises.

"Stop it with the cowboy mentality," scolded Apollo. "Look," he said to me, "I wanted to talk to you, and Mr. Impulsive over here had to come along and share his silly opinions. That's why I had Zeus make him use the rubber ducky."

"I wanted the ducky!" insisted Dionysus.

"Did not."

"Did too."

"Did not."

"Double did too."

"Come on, guys, stop it!" I yelled.

"Sorry," offered Apollo. "Look, you are in grave danger. I'm here to remind you that you would be taking too great a risk if you ran those upcoming rapids in this canoe. You don't have flotation bags or a spray skirt. You don't know how high the water is, either. And I don't think I have to remind you that you are only an *intermediate* canoeist—not an expert. It's time to park the canoe and walk around the rapids."

"There he goes again," taunted Dionysus. He was lying on his back, resting his flowing Greek-god locks tumbling into the water. He had one hand trailing carelessly through the water.

"OK, wise guy," said Apollo, "why don't you tell me what *you* think?" Then he whispered to me, "That shouldn't take long."

"Heard that!" said Dionysus. "Hey, life can get really dull. You have to live it up when you can, right? Just look at those rapids! You know you want to crouch down in the canoe and let 'er rip—you know, just catch the rush of it all!"

In the back of the canoe, Apollo imitated Dionysus. "You know, just catch the rush of it all, dude, you know?" he mocked in an exaggerated surfer's accent.

"Oh, shut up, killjoy!" replied Dionysus. "You're just jealous because the ladies would rather worship me."

"Dream on," snorted Apollo. He turned back to me. "Don't listen to the skipper of the good ship Rubber Ducky. He's always getting you mortals into trouble with all the loud parties and and other shenanigans."

"*Shenanigans*?" laughed Dionysus. "My stars! You sound like my grandmother."

"Oh, be *quiet!*" snapped Apollo. "You see? He'd rather make fun of my vocabulary than actually disagree with my reasoning. He knows that I'm telling the truth, but he thinks that he will lose all of his charm if he shows any maturity. I'm here to tell you that you need to be *careful*. Don't tempt the Sisters of Fate. I know those ladies, and they have issues—let's just say that they don't handle power very well. Anyway, you mere mortals don't know what's in store for you."

"Do *you* know what's in store for me?" I asked. "Because those rapids are coming up, and maybe just this once, I'd kind of like to listen to Dionysus."

"Well," Dionysus said, "he knows what's in store for you, but you can't get him to tell you. Apollo *could* warn you, but he'd rather just blame the Sisters of Fate. If you do get killed, he'll chatter on for hours about how you didn't have to die, and about how he gave you *specific rules* to follow that could have convinced the gods to be on your side, and about how this whole big mess could have been avoided. Hanging out with him gets to be a real drag."

"Do *you* know if I should take the rapids?" I asked.

"Where's the thrill in knowing whether something is safe?" asked Dionysus.

I was going to respond, but the air suddenly exploded with a violent, blinding bolt of lightning. When the smoke cleared, I saw Jared sitting in the back of the canoe, right where Apollo had been. I glanced to the right and saw that Dionysus was gone, too. "What's the matter?" Jared asked. "You look like you just saw a ghost or something."

I wanted to tell him, but the rapids were so close that I could hear them roaring. "Jared," I warned, "we'd better pull over and carry around these rapids!"

"Why?" Jared asked. "These are usually a Class II."

"But the water could be too high, don't you think?" I asked. "You know, we mortals never know what may happen."

Jared gave me a quizzical look. "What are you worried about?" he asked. Pulling a yellow rubber ducky from the pocket of his lifejacket, he joked, "This will save us if we get dumped!"

Questions

1. Have you ever had to make a quick decision like the canoeist in the story? What did you do?

2. In situations like this, would you be more likely to listen to Apollo, or Dionysus?

3. What are the benefits of listening to Apollo? What are the benefits of listening to Dionysus?

4. Does the narrator have a Dionysian or an Apollonian personality? How about his friend Jared? Explain why you answered the way you did.

Apollonian vs. Dionysian Character Study

Book: _____

Author: _____

On the scale below, indicate whether the protagonist (main character) of this book has more of an Apollonian temperament or a Dionysian one. If there are two or more main characters, then write their names in the appropriate spots on the scale.

←—————————————————————————————————————→

Dionysian	**More Dionysian**	**Shows Both Equally**	**More Apollonian**	**Apollonian**
Impulsive,				Cautious,
Emotional,				Rational,
Spontaneous,				Restrained,
Takes Risks				Prudent

Answer the following questions in full sentences, using additional paper if you need it.

1. Explain why you classified the character(s) the way you did.

_____

_____

_____

_____

_____

2. If the main character begins the book with a Dionysian temperament, what events in the story challenge him or her to become more Apollonian? Likewise, if the main character is more Apollonian, what events in the story challenge him or her to become more Dionysian? (If there is more than one main character, choose only one character to write about.)

_____

_____

_____

_____

_____

3. If the main character does not change at all, explain why.

_____

_____

_____

_____

_____

_____

4. Describe the major risks the protagonist has to take throughout the story.

_____

_____

_____

_____

_____

_____

5. Describe how the character's life changes after he or she takes these risks.

_____

_____

_____

_____

_____

_____

6. What does the protagonist learn from these decisions and experiences?

_____

_____

_____

_____

_____

_____

Dissecting a Decision

Think back to an important decision you made fairly recently. Analyze your decision using the table below. Give your decision a creative title, and use additional paper if you need it.

Decision:
What was the decision you made?
What was the alternative (what could you have done instead)?

What would have been safe about choosing the alternative?	What would have been the risks of choosing the alternative?
What was safe about your choice?	What was risky about your choice?

Evaluation Criteria

Playing It Safe or Going for Broke, Shopping With Friends and Plastic, and **Paddling With the Toga Boys** were written to inspire discussion and journaling. It is up to you whether to assign grades for these activities. You may decide to use the Discussion Evaluation slip provided on page 10. If you instruct students to write formal responses to the provided questions, you might create a rubric or grade the responses according to whatever guidelines you provide your students.

For **Apollonian vs. Dionysian Character Study**, you should focus on the student's justifications for classifying characters in literature. (To tweak this assignment, you may wish to allow students to analyze films; they are often more excited about applying what they've learned to works with which they are more familiar.) Students should use full sentences and back up their points.

Dissecting a Decision requires students to be candid and opens the door for many very personal responses. If you decide to conduct a discussion of students' responses—which may be a very interesting and insightful discussion—it is best to avoid cold calling on students, allowing them instead to volunteer. Their responses should be well written and should demonstrate insight and reflection.

CHAPTER
12

Melting Pot vs. Melting Not

Objectives

⚙ Students will identify and classify actions as being characteristic of either identity or assimilation.

⚙ Students will analyze the respective impacts of identity and assimilation, as opposing tensions, within and between American culture(s).

⚙ Students will appraise the merits of identity and assimilation.

⚙ Students will create questions that assess the presence or absence of a common culture.

Introduction

I recall looking out from the gardens of the Alhambra, the famous Moorish palace in Granada, Spain, on a summer afternoon in 1986. Below me, I could see the historic Jewish and Christian sectors of the town. The Moors, devoted Muslims, were noted for encouraging dialogue among scholars from all three faiths. Later in the same summer, I rode a bus through the streets of Tangiers and saw French automobiles, Spanish businessmen, Taureg tribesmen, imams, shaggy European backpackers, and Moroccan merchants all weaving their way through open-air markets. America is not the only country that has faced the challenges and rewards of pluralism. However, given our complicated history of liberty and enslavement, along with the belief that our country is a "melting pot," America seems to have been uniquely tested by the ideal of forming a perfect union.

Many Americans repeat stories about their ancestry that become more and more muddled with each rendition. Many of these stories follow a familiar plot: Following years of poverty, oppression, or both, impoverished ancestors boarded a ship bound for America. After leaving Ellis Island, they worked hard to get ahead. Eventually, their small business or farm became successful enough for them to make a better life for their children. The children of these immigrants then got a good education and established themselves in more illustrious careers, leaving their ethnic identities behind and joining the melting pot of America. This is a classic story of assimilation, in which one group adopts the cultural traits of the larger society that its members have joined.

As with any mythical story, the plot outlined in the previous paragraph has some truth to it. However, the story doesn't hold true for many descendants of African slaves, conquered Native American tribes, Hispanic people whose land was stolen by the United States in the Mexican-American war, or Asian immigrants who were promised labor but denied rights as citizens.

Furthermore, the assimilation story does not apply to countless individuals who have elected to retain some or all of their particular ethnic identity. This does not necessarily mean that these people have rejected mainstream American society. Instead, they have decided to participate on their own terms and in their own fashion, maintaining the mores, practices, and other aspects of their ethnicities and cultures.

Some groups actively and violently reject American society and mainstream assimilation. The most radical separatist groups are motivated by ideologies, incendiary rhetoric, and hatred towards other races. For example, both Keystone United (a skinhead, White power organization) and the New Black Panther Party have been listed on the Southern Poverty Law Center's (2011) online list of national hate groups. It is ironic that although members of these groups would not be found in a room together, they find themselves rubbing elbows on a list of national hatemongers.

Although hate groups garner national attention, the vast majority of the population does not endorse extremists or even come into contact

with them. Far down the scale from extremism is a mindset that supports ethnic identity while advocating for peaceful participation in society. Many Americans will refer to this orientation as promoting diversity, while others may criticize it as "playing politics" with identity. The meaning of the terms varies with the context and intent of the speaker. It is in this realm—the political realm—that we most often encounter tension between ethnic identity and assimilation.

An example of such ethnic tension recently occurred in Oklahoma. In 2004, a Muslim schoolgirl was suspended for wearing a hijab, a traditional scarf, to class. Her family brought a lawsuit against the district and won the case ("U.S. to Defend Muslim Girl," 2004). France also made international headlines with its debates over banning Muslim scarves as "conspicuous religious symbols" in state schools ("Headscarf Defeat," 2005).

Almost two decades ago, Arthur Schlesinger (1992) wrote a small, controversial book entitled *The Disuniting of America.* Schlesinger openly challenged many of the popular manifestations of multiculturalism in the public domain, especially public education. In particular, he branded some Afrocentric curricula as historically inaccurate and ideologically divisive. He also criticized many elite academics for instinctively dismissing the Western canon of literature as merely a collection of works designed to support dominant classes. At the end of his book, Schlesinger stated,

> Our task is to combine due appreciation of the splendid diversity of the nation with due emphasis on the great unifying Western ideas of individual freedom, political democracy, and human rights. These are the ideas that define the American nationality—and that today empower people of all continents, races, and creeds. (p. 138)

Schlesinger was obviously in favor of assimilation, the melting pot philosophy wherein all citizens take on the same values and characteristics. For him, people could "melt" into a common identity by sharing the universal values of our national culture. P. D. Salins (1997), a professor of urban planning at Hunter College, also warned of the balkanization of America by separatist ideologues. He too suggested that there was more to gain for all ethnic groups in America by embracing a common national culture typified by values like those described by Schlesinger.

Of course, not all people agree with the idea that America can embrace everyone within a common set of cultural values. Advocates for minority groups contend that while we may have moved beyond the obvious discriminatory practices that inspired the Civil Rights Movement, we are still beleaguered by more subtle biases within dominant social institutions such as banks, schools, and healthcare organizations. The term *institutional racism* has been used to describe these more abstract, indirect forms of discrimination. Many Americans support inclusion policies (e.g., affirmative action) as a means of combating institutional racism. Critics of these policies accuse ethnic groups of playing the race card, using reverse discrimination, and endorsing identity politics.

Many multicultural education programs support a more positive view of separatism among minority cultures than those that have been put forth by Schlesinger (1992), Salins (1997), and critics of inclusion policies. Instead of considering the nation a melting pot, multicultural educators often use the metaphor of a tapestry. These theorists propose that ethnicities weave together, rather than melt into a single entity, to create the fiber of American life. From this perspective, ethnic identity may be retained—whether out of choice or by necessity—and people can still participate in common national goals. What can ultimately be said about ethnic identity in our country? Simply put, it is messy, and it always has been. The opposition of melting pot vs. melting not is ripe for critical discussion. It is important to resist jumping to any conclusions, and it is difficult to separate out what we have been told to believe, rather than exploring all of the relevant issues and coming to our own informed decisions. Within such passionate and highly personal subject areas, it is tempting to be suspicious of and angry at people who hold opposing views; nevertheless, it is important to remember that on both sides of this debate, as with all debates, there are people who have good intentions. Melting pot advocates (like Schlesinger) do not necessarily wish to ignore racism or minimize the rights of various ethnic groups. Likewise, identity advocates are not necessarily pushing for radical separation or playing the race card, as their detractors often claim. It is vital to examine these opposing parties' intentions and histories. Well-intentioned individuals on both sides want what is best; they simply offer different solutions for how best to live in a pluralist society.

Finally, it is critical to acknowledge the necessity of addressing the tensions between assimilation and cultural identity. Constructive, respectful dialogue will allow us to resolve differences while sustaining the promise of a brighter future for everybody. We cannot remain silent about the tensions between assimilation (melting pot) and cultural identity. Constructive, respectful dialogue will allow us to resolve differences while sustaining the promise of justice for everyone. As President Barack Obama (2008) explained in "A More Perfect Union," his now-famous speech on race, remaining silent about the issues that have divided America will not help us progress—we must talk about them.

Classroom Activities and Assessments

What I Was Taught (p. 196) is a reflection and journaling activity designed to encourage students to explore how the topics of ethnic identity and assimilation were presented or modeled to them as they grew up. These responses could be discussed, but you may opt to assure students that their responses will be kept private, serving primarily to prepare them for class discussion later on. **Investigation Poster** (p. 197; rubric on p. 203) requires students to create a poster on a topic dealing with cultural/ethnic identity or conflict. Each poster must reflect research on the chosen topic, and students are expected to present their posters and topics to classmates. Poster presentations may be organized as individual speeches, seminar sessions accompanied by short speeches, or "museum walks," wherein the posters are displayed and students circulate looking at them. You may grade students' presentations if you wish, and a rubric for the poster is provided, to which you may apply your own point values and grading criteria. **Do We Have a National Culture?** (p. 200; teacher guide on p. 198) is a survey project designed to allow students to investigate whether or not respondents seem to share a common set of core American values. The questions in the survey were developed using the seven central values of mainstream American culture proposed in *American Culture: Myth and Reality of a Culture of Diversity*, by anthropologist Larry Naylor (1998). Students must also add their own questions to the survey and justify the rationale for their questions. Once they have collected data, they tabulate, report, and analyze their results. You may wish to use the set of analysis questions provided in the **Survey Analysis** (pp. 201–202; rubric on p. 204), or you can come up with your own. If you wish, you can expand upon this assignment to make it an interdisciplinary project by increasing the focus on statistical measures and research design.

What I Was Taught

Please carefully reflect on and answer the following questions. Your responses will not be collected, but you may wish to draw on them during class discussion. These questions refer to what you learned as a child, from the adults around you, about American society and ethnicity. As you consider your responses, keep in mind that adults teach children through both words and actions.

1. What did adults teach you about your own ethnicity?

   _____

   _____

   _____

   _____

   _____

   _____

2. What did adults teach you about other ethnic groups?

   _____

   _____

   _____

   _____

   _____

   _____

3. Were you raised with a concept of America as a "melting pot"? If so, how did this affect your vision of America? If not, were you taught to think about America in some other way?

   _____

   _____

   _____

   _____

   _____

   _____

Investigation Poster

Prompt

You will be responsible for investigating an issue, topic, or conflict situation that is rooted in the tension between ethnic/cultural identity and cultural assimilation. Your investigation may focus on historical or current material from anywhere in the world. Examples of possible topics include early Spanish missions in Mexico, ethnic conflict in the Balkans, past immigration laws, bilingual education, Native American opinions on Columbus Day, Afrocentric vs. Eurocentric education, current conflict in Sudan, separatist tendencies of the Amish, and Hasidic Jews in America. Make sure that you focus on the debate between assimilating and maintaining identity, rather than on racism or bigotry—this topic deserves much attention as well, but it is not the subject of this assignment.

Requirements

Your poster should be on standard poster paper. It should contain the following:

- A one-page summary on the topic. The summary must be single-spaced, sized 12-point font, and free from errors in spelling, capitalization, usage, and punctuation.

- A title, a border, and at least three illustrations, maps, diagrams, charts, and so forth. Each illustration should have a caption. Illustrations may be graphs, drawings, or photographs. The poster should be neat, and any text you use should be typed.

- A bibliography taped or glued to the back, formatted in an approved style. You must use a minimum of three sources (this is in addition to any websites you use to find pictures or illustrations.)

Your investigation poster should offer a general overview of the topic you have chosen. Avoid getting lost in less important details. Your poster must be informative, as well as neat and eye catching.

Do We Have a National Culture?

Teacher Guidelines

The primary purpose of this lesson is to stimulate students' thinking about the opposing forces of cultural assimilation and identity. Students will need to distribute a survey, evaluate its results, and arrive at conclusions.

Objectives

- ⚙ Students will synthesize conclusions from multiple sources.
- ⚙ Students will understand the ways in which assimilation and identity shape values and opinions.

Instructions

1. After teaching students about the essential features of the identity vs. assimilation opposition, distribute the Do We Have a National Culture Survey and instruction sheets on page 200.

2. Assign students to work in pairs or small groups. Explain that although they will be working together, each student will be responsible for his or her own individual work.

3. Explain that the survey is designed to assess whether (and if so, to what degree) there is a true "American" culture.

4. Tell students that they will be distributing this survey to respondents (you decide how many surveys each student has to distribute).

5. Instruct students to come up with three original questions for their surveys. These will serve as items 8, 9, and 10 on the survey. (Students working in pairs must have identical questions, so they must settle on three questions to appear on their joint survey.)

6. When they receive the returned surveys, they will analyze the results and respond to the Do We Have a National Culture Survey Analysis sheet on pages 201–202. Results will be shared and discussed in class.

7. Ensure that students understand the survey so that they can explain it to respondents and correctly interpret the results. A response of "Always" indicates general agreement with the value presented in the survey question. The questions that students

generate should be posed in the same way, so that an answer of "Always" will consistently mean that the respondent agrees with the value being asked about.

8. Review students' responses on the Survey Analysis sheet.

9. It is a good idea to monitor students as they create survey items and to conference with students before any large-group discussion, as some items and answers could be controversial.

Survey Etiquette

Remind students that survey responses are to be anonymous and voluntary. Survey respondents do not have to justify their answers. Also, remind students that when reporting results, they must use neutral, inoffensive language. They should analyze the results, but they should not express either positive or negative opinions about them.

Do We Have a National Culture?

Age: _____ Sex: _____ Race/Ethnicity: _____ Political Affiliation: _____

Please complete the following survey by indicating whether you think each statement is never true, rarely true, usually true, or always true. Try to answer thoughtfully and honestly; your answers and identity will be kept confidential. Thank you for your participation in this survey.

1. Americans are hard workers.

    Never   Rarely   Usually   Always

2. Americans treat each other equally.

    Never   Rarely   Usually   Always

3. Americans are independent and do not follow others.

    Never   Rarely   Usually   Always

4. Americans are able to change their lives for the better.

    Never   Rarely   Usually   Always

5. Americans support freedom of speech.

    Never   Rarely   Usually   Always

6. If an American wants to, he or she can be successful.

    Never   Rarely   Usually   Always

7. Americans are honest.

    Never   Rarely   Usually   Always

8. _____

    Never   Rarely   Usually   Always

9. _____

    Never   Rarely   Usually   Always

10. _____

    Never   Rarely   Usually   Always

Do We Have a National Culture?

Survey Analysis

In the space provided, list the three additional items (8, 9, and 10) you chose to include, and explain why you included each. Use additional paper if you need more space.

Survey item 8 and reasoning:

_____

_____

_____

_____

_____

_____

_____

Survey item 9 and reasoning:

_____

_____

_____

_____

_____

_____

_____

Survey item 10 and reasoning:

_____

_____

_____

_____

_____

_____

_____

Next, follow the steps below to analyze the findings of your survey.

1. Assign a numeric value of 0 to 4 to each item response (e.g., "Never" is worth 0, and "Always" is worth 4) and calculate the average point value per survey item.

Item 1: _____   Item 6: _____

Item 2: _____   Item 7: _____

Item 3: _____   Item 8: _____

Item 4: _____   Item 9: _____

Item 5: _____   Item 10: _____

2. Present the results on a separate sheet of paper. You should create a table, a graph, or some other type of organized method of showing your results.

3. Discuss the results. On a separate sheet of paper, write several paragraphs, including the following information:

   a) Overall, what do you think the results you obtained mean?
   b) Describe how the results may support or oppose the concept of a shared American culture.
   c) Were there differences in how people responded to the survey based on their age, sex, race/ethnicity, or political party? If so, how might you explain these differences?
   d) After conducting your survey, can you arrive at any conclusions, or are there questions you could research further? What are they?

Name: _____ Date: _____

Investigation Poster

Rubric

	Poor	Adequate	Excellent
Summary (content)	Coverage disorganized or inadequate.	Essential information present.	Summary concise and comprehensive.
Summary (mechanics)	Numerous errors disrupt summary's flow.	Summary contains few errors; flow not disrupted.	Summary contains no errors.
Title and border	Information handwritten; title or border missing.	Title and border present.	Title and border reflect subject area and major themes.
Illustrations	One or more illustrations missing or poorly related to the topic; one or more captions handwritten.	Contains at least three relevant illustrations with typed captions.	Contains three or more illustrations with typed captions; illustrations aid understanding of topic.
Bibliography	Lists fewer than three sources; not formatted in approved style.	Lists three or more sources; formatted in approved style.	Lists three or more complicated and comprehensive sources; formatted in approved style.

Comments:

_____

_____

_____

Do We Have a National Culture? Survey Analysis

Rubric

Rationale for original items	Inadequate or incomplete	Inconsistent, unclear	Accurate, clear	Insightful, creative
Presentation of results	Inadequate or incomplete	Inconsistent, unclear	Accurate, clear	Organized, professional
Discussion of results	Inadequate or incomplete	Inconsistent, unclear	Accurate, clear	Fluent, accurate
Analysis and conclusions	Inadequate or incomplete	Inconsistent, unclear	Accurate, clear	Insightful, original
Overall organization	Poor	Adequate	Good	Excellent

Comments:

_____

_____

_____

References

Allitt, P. (2009). *The conservatives: Ideas and attitudes throughout American history*. New Haven, CT: Yale University Press.

Bainbridge, D. (2009). *Teenagers: A natural history*. Vancouver, British Columbia: Greystone Books.

Bouchard, T. J. (1999). Genes, environment, and personality. In S. J. Ceci & W. M. Williams (Eds.), *The nature-nurture debate: The essential readings* (pp. 98–103). Malden, MA: Blackwell.

Brown, M. B. (1995). *Models in political economy: A guide to the arguments* (2nd ed). London, UK: Penguin Books.

Caporaso, J. A., & Levine, D. P. (1992). *Theories of political economy*. Cambridge, UK: Cambridge University Press.

Carter, R., & Frith, C. D. (2000). *Mapping the mind*. Berkeley: University of California Press.

Cohen, M., & Nagel, E. (1976). Scientific method. In M. M. Rader & J. H. Gill (Eds.), *The enduring questions: Main problems of philosophy* (3rd ed., pp. 217–226). New York, NY: Holt, Rinehart, and Winston.

College Student Credit Card. (2008). *Credit card statistics*. Retrieved from http://www.collegestudentcreditcard.com/articles11.html

Cook, J. W. (1999). *Morality and cultural differences*. New York, NY: Oxford University Press.

Culham, R. (2003). *6 + 1 traits of writing: The complete guide*. New York, NY: Scholastic Professional Books.

Dawkins, R. (2006). *The selfish gene*. New York, NY: Oxford University Press.

Edkins, J. (2007). *Fibonacci numbers and the golden ratio*. Retrieved from http://gwydir.demon.co.uk/jo/numbers/interest/golden

Engels, F. (1891). Introduction to wage, labour and capital. In International Publishers (Eds.), *Karl Marx and Frederick Engels selected works* (pp. 64–94). New York, NY: International Publishers.

Foreman, J. (2009, June 22). Dear, I love you with all my brain. *The Los Angeles Times*. Retrieved from http://articles.latimes.com/2009/jun/22/health/he-love22

Gene transfer enhances pair bonding in monogamous voles. (2001, September 17). *ScienceDaily*. Retrieved from http://www.sciencedaily.com/releases/2001/09/010917075347.htm

Gottfredson, L. S. (2002). Gottfredson's theory of circumscription, compromise, and self-creation. In D. Brown & Associates (Eds.), *Career choice and development* (4th ed., pp. 85–148). San Francisco, CA: Jossey-Bass.

Gupta, S. (2002, February 2). The chemistry of love. *Time Magazine*. Retrieved from http://www.time.com/time/magazine/article/0,9171,1101020218-201904,00.html

Hamilton, E. (1942). *Mythology: Timeless tales of gods and heroes*. New York, NY: Grand Central Publishing.

Headscarf defeat riles French Muslims. (2005, November 1). *BBC News*. Retrieved from http://news.bbc.co.uk/2/hi/europe/4395934.stm

Hirsch, E. D., Kett, J. F., & Trefil, J. (2002). *The new dictionary of cultural literacy*. Boston, MA: Houghton Mifflin Company.

Holowchak, A. M. (2007). *Critical reasoning and science: Looking at science with an investigative eye*. Lanham, MD: University Press of America.

Hopfe, L. M. (1994). *Religions of the world* (6th ed.). New York, NY: Macmillan.

Horadum, A. F. (1975). *800 years young*. Retrieved from http://faculty.evansville.edu/ck6/bstud/fibo.html

Jones, W. T. (1970). *A history of Western philosophy: The classical mind* (2nd ed.). New York, NY: Harcourt, Brace, & Jovanovich.

Livio, M. (2009). *Is God a mathematician?* New York, NY: Simon and Schuster.

Locke, J. (1976). *An essay concerning human understanding*. In M. Rader (Ed.), *The enduring questions: Main problems of philosophy* (3rd ed., pp. 168–189). New York, NY: Holt, Rinehart, & Winston. (Original work published 1690)

Marx, K., & Engels, F. (1848). Manifesto of the communist party. In International Publishers (Eds.), *Karl Marx and Frederick Engels selected works* (pp. 31–63). New York, NY: International Publishers.

Naylor, L. L. (1998). *American culture: Myth and reality of a culture of diversity*. Westport, CT: Bergin and Garvey.

Nietzsche, F. (1967). *The birth of tragedy* (W. Kaufmann, Trans.). New York, NY: Vintage Books. (Original work published 1886)

O'Neill, W. F. (1981). *Educational ideologies*. Santa Monica, CA: Goodyear.

Obama, B. H. (2008, Mar. 18). *A more perfect union*. Speech given at the National Constitution Center, Philadelphia, PA.

Parry, R. (2007). Epistemology. *Stanford Dictionary of Philosophy*. Retrieved from http://plato.stanford.edu

Pines, M. (2008). *A secret sense in the human nose: Sniffing out social and sexual signals*. http://www.hhmi.org/senses/d210.html

Robinson, D., & Garratt, C. (1996). *Ethics: A graphic guide*. Cambridge, UK: Totem Books.

Rothman, T., & Sudarshan, G. (1998). *Doubt and certainty*. Cambridge, MA: Perseus Books.

Russell, B. (1954). *A history of Western philosophy*. New York, NY: Simon and Schuster.

Rutter, M. (2006). *Genes and behavior: Nature-nurture interplay explained*. Malden, MA: Blackwell.

Sahakian, W. S. (1968). *History of philosophy*. New York, NY: HarperCollins.

Salins, P. D. (1997). *Assimilation, American style*. New York, NY: Basic Books.

Schick, T., & Vaughn, L. (2008). *How to think about weird things*. New York, NY: McGraw Hill.

Schlesinger, A. M. (1992). *The disuniting of America: Reflections on a multicultural society*. New York, NY: W. W. Norton and Company.

Schnitzer, M. C. (1991). *Comparative economic systems*. Cincinatti, OH: South-Western Publishing.

Self-control, and lack of self-control, is contagious. (2010, January 18). *ScienceDaily*. Retrieved from http://www.sciencedaily.com/releases/2010/01/100113172359.htm

Shapiro, S. (2000). *Thinking about mathematics*. Oxford, UK: Oxford University Press.

Skinner, B. F. (1971). *Beyond freedom and dignity*. Indianapolis, IN: Hackett.

Skinner, B. F. (1975). *Walden two*. New York, NY: Macmillan.

Sowell, T. (2006). *On classical economics*. New Haven, CT: Yale University Press.

Southern Poverty Law Center. (2011). *Groups*. Retrieved from http://www.splcenter.org/get-informed/intelligence-files/groups

Spillius, A. (2001, February 25). Borneo killings drive out settlers. *Telegraph*. Retrieved from http://www.telegraph.co.uk/news/worldnews/asia/indonesia/1324109/Borneo-killings-drive-out-settlers.html

Stumpf, S. E. (1983). *Philosophy: History and problems* (3rd ed.). New York, NY: McGraw-Hill.

Tasler, N. (2008). *The impulse factor*. New York, NY: Fireside Books.

Temptation more powerful than individuals realize. (2009, August 4). *ScienceDaily*. Retrieved from http://www.sciencedaily.com/releases/2009/08/090803132746.htm

Tuchman, B. W. (1978). *A distant mirror: The calamitous 14th century*. New York, NY: Ballantine.

Valens, E. G. (1964). *The number of things: Pythagoras, geometry and humming strings*. New York, NY: E. P. Dutton.

United Nations. (1948). *The Universal Declaration of Human Rights*. Retrieved from http://www.un.org/en/documents/udhr/

U.S. to defend Muslim girl wearing scarf in school. (2004, March 30). *CNN Justice*. Retrieved from http://articles.cnn.com/2004-03-30/justice/us.school.headscarves_1_dress-code-head-scarf-muslim-head-scarves?_s=PM:LAW

White, J. E. (1997). *Contemporary moral problems* (5th ed.). Minneapolis, MN: West Publishing Company.

Wynn, C. M., & Wiggins, A. W. (2001). *Quantum leaps in the wrong direction*. Washington, DC: Joseph Henry Press.

About the Authors

Clark G. Porter, Ph.D., teaches gifted and talented middle school students in Waterloo, IA. He has received state and regional awards for his teaching. Dr. Porter has worked as a school psychologist, nonprofit administrator, adjunct university instructor, and teacher.

James M. Girsch, Ph.D., studied natural science and languages at the University of Iowa, and he holds an M.A. and a Ph.D. in Medieval Latin and English literature from the University of Toronto's Centre for Medieval Studies. He did graduate coursework in architecture at the University of Michigan. In addition to teaching history, literature, writing, and Latin, he has worked as a lexicographer, translator, writer, and editor.